ARTIA

CZECH
ARCHITECTURE
OF THE
LUXEMBURG
PERIOD

VÁCLAV MENCL

CZECH
ARCHITECTURE
OF THE
LUXEMBURG
PERIOD

*

ARTIA – PRAGUE

VÁCLAV MENCL

CZECH ARCHITECTURE OF THE LUXEMBURG PERIOD

TRANSLATED BY L. KOLLMANNOVÁ

INTRODUCTION

Bohemia has been preparing for its historical task ever since the earliest beginnings of its artistic production. It entered the history of art as early as the tenth century when the foundations of block-in-shape style were being laid in Central Europe. At that period Saxony stood at the head of Germany attempting to create a new style; in the latter part of the tenth century large basilicae of elaborate ground-plans were built at Gernrode (961—83), at Quedlinburg (986—1017) and circa 1.000 at Hildesheim. Although their interiors were focussed upon the altars they remained in the hold of compact surrounding walls and all apertures were simply cut out in them. On the exterior, however, we may trace the first suggestions of storeys which is the earliest manner of arcticulation.

If we follow these beginnings in Bohemia it is obvious that Czech architecture will adopt artistic forms of its own based on domestic spiritual resources. During the first hundred years of its development there appears a very characteristic type of architecture, namely the Czech rotunda. It is true that it followed the example of a foreign model, that of the Wenceslas Church at the Prague Castle (St. Vitus Church, cons. in 930), but there were other models available too, for example, the block-in-shape churches of longitudinal ground-plans. The selection of a central type had, therefore, deeper reasons than to satisfy the needs. Rotunda is, namely, for the most part a spatial formation; the starting-point of its form is its inner space enveloped by the building shell. Thus arose a strange, compact block of mass inconvenient, especially for the vaults, as there are no right angles to be found within it. It would be very daring nowadays to search for the pedigree of the Czech rotunda; it would take us back to late Roman architecture. Immediately at the beginning of their artistic development the Czechs became familiar with its central types as they were easily comprehensible and spiritually near, giving rise to impulse and inspiration.

The invasion of western spirit as represented by the Benedictine monastic churches, and at a subsequent period by the Cistercian and Premonstratensian orders, put an end to Czech rotunda. Czech art was subortinated to the West for three centuries. German conception of building in blocks of compact mass, which envelopes interiors resembling caves, pervaded the oldest Czech basilica, St. George's at the Prague Castle (after 1000), as well as the youngest one at Milevsko (circa 1200) which in spite of its late date could hardly be distinguished from any block-in-shape building of Otonian time. This style may be traced in the provinces of Bohemia as late as the Sixties of the thirteenth century.

There were, of course, some exceptions, too: as early as 1165 there occurred in St. James near Kuttenberg a west front covered with blind arcades containing sculptured details. The façade followed the model of Ratisbon, while the blind arcading was of Poitven type. The arcade of Rhenish-Lombardian style was applied to the monastic church at Doksany circa 1220—30 and only ten years afterwards the Saxon style of Königsluter type may be traced in the Vinec group of churches which bear the first signs of tectonic order. These were but isolated cases; on the whole Czech churches were still block-shaped.

Radical change was not brought about until the Thirties of the thirteenth century. At that period there appeared in Bohemia a group of buildings whose style was younger by at least three hundred years than the entire local architecture. Foreign style brought along by German colonists suddenly pervaded Bohemia. Building operations were directed by foreigners who began to realise artistic ideals completely alien to the Czech spirit. At the head of the German invasions stood the Cistercian Order, supplying models of Burgundian and Swabian monasteries established circa 1210 at Maulbronn. Churches and monasteries at Osek, Hradiště, Nepomuk, Tišnov and Velehrad of which the oldest parts belong to the period of 1230—50, recall the advanced Gothic architecture of Burgundy whose supply of forms spread so quickly throughout Bohemia that about the middle of the century it provided the basis for stylistic forms of the entire foreign architecture whether they were direct building operations of the King (the castles of Zvíkov and Písek), of his towns (the parish Church at Písek, monastic churches at Brno, Jihlava and in Prague), or finally country churches. This rapid expansion may be explained in that it was not the actual French Gothic but a style derived from the tectonic principles of Burgundy that came into consideration here; although ribbed vaults and clustered shafts were applied throughout the building, the case was not a true articulation of the wall to which sham-tectonic forms were merely added. And so under the sham-Gothic scaffolding there survived the plain mass of walls or piers as the individual columns attached to it could easily be removed, forming but superfluous additions. It is obvious that these pseudo-tectonic forms of Cistercian style were produced even in Bohemia for their own sake, composing the tectonic structure of a building in a similar manner as a child plays with its toy-blocks. Thus it was a massive block that represented the proper sense of a building, adopting new style to local environments and causing Bohemia to deny the accomplished tectonic forms of Northern France for a long time. The old domestic attitude towards matter was further strengthened when the Cistercians themselves set their vaults on simple corbels or at least terminated the shortened bars of the engaged shafts in a corbel-like manner so that the actual wall remained untouched by the tectonic consequences of the vaulting.

The invasion of the High Gothic style which circa 1260 followed that of Cistercian Gothic was met with such fierce resistence in Bohemia that the tectonic articulation of a building did not occur at all. It is true that in some pseudo-tectonic structures a free column of Cistercian type was replaced by a tripartite shaft of Rheims origin modelled after the example of the church at Marburg, yet the Church of St. Barbara in Prague, as well as the parish churches at Kolín and Kouřim commenced in this new style, assumed a block-in-shape form of Saxonian type immediately after the departure of their original builders who had founded them. Local architecture of Bohemia resisted French tectonic forms in several ways, the most effective being their application to Cistercian systems of forms wherein they expired (the chapels at Zvíkov and Horšovský Týn with shafts set on corbels, the passageway at Křivoklát, where under the clustered columns the massive form of a pier survives), or to those of Saxony (the Chapel at Bezděz). Very soon, however, reduction was attained here. So early as 1280 simple bars were employed in place of tripartite shafts of classic type as exemplified in the Old-New Synagogue in Prague, while circa 1300 these simplified shafts are no longer apt to dominate the surface of walls. At first it was the Cistercian style of Burgundy and then the Central-European tendencies of reduction that maintained the old artistic purpose of block-in-shape form, even if it assumed a vertical character.

The forms of a subsequent stylistic stage, German expressionism, brought to Bohemia by the Cistercian Order have also been simplified and made fully massive by reduction. Circa 1300 or shortly before large Cistercian buildings were carried out at Zlatá Koruna (the Chapter-Hall and the eastern part of the church) and at Nepomuk, where plastic detail was freely employed (poppyheads, columned piers, panelling, finials) following contemporary France. The French vaulting system was, however, so simplified here that in place of shafts running uninterruptedly from the pavement under the vaulting there are simple corbels split into several projecting parts. It is still the old wall of Cistercian type as is also apparent in the choir of the church at Budějovice, belonging to the Dominican Order and modelled on that of Zlatá Koruna where the clustered shafts are again placed on corbels. This reduction was further continued so that in the choir of the parish church at Horažďovice the style returned back to block-in-shape form; the aisles are even destitute of vaulting ribs. Similarly also the linear shafts of Čáslav Church (from about 1300) were merely plain-chamfered. At a subsequent period we find these shafts even within the most accomplished structures of Gothic expressionism, in the choirs of the parish churches at Plzeň and in Prague (St. Mary-in-the-Snow). Incessant return to a compact massive body and to simple, inarticulated surface formed the most important feature of Czech expressionism, also providing the reason why Czech Gothic architecture did not follow the spiritual constructions of French style and why the Czech art of building had to be content with a mere vertical tendency of proportions even at a period of its most intense spiritual effort.

As early as 1330 Bohemia was prepared to initiate the development of late Gothic style. The process of reduction had just reached its climax with the three large churches of aisled halls: St. Bartolomew at Plzeň, St. Giles in Prague and St. Nicolas at Znojmo in Moravia. Within all of them the shaft is completely absorbed by the wall so that the interiors are enveloped by a single, in all its parts uniform and massive body. The building mass is displayed symmetrically for the buttressing piers were incorporated into the wall of which the apertures were again simply cut out, in no way spoiling its uniform character; in a similar manner interior space absorbed the vaulting compartments which almost disappeared in it. With these churches the aim of style has been attained, the building was changed into a compact body as in the period of Romanesque style. Such a body, though once Gothicized, shows but slight evidence of Gothic tectonic principles; as against the actual structures of Romanesque style it has retained a Gothic, vertical tendency next to the capacity for sensitive reaction to external impulses which allowed it to take a part in further stylistic processes.

We notice that circa 1330 a late Gothic process based on optic principles was commenced in Bohemia. Fostered by Czech sensualism, it soon distinguished Czech architecture from the rest of European building operations, having imparted a truly Czech character upon it.

THE HISTORY OF CZECH GOTHIC ARCHITECTURE

We shall begin our description of Czech Gothic architecture with St. James' Church at Kuttenberg. The town, founded in the last twenty years of the thirteenth century, has so far been consolidated in the Twenties of the fourteenth century that the choir of the parish church, dedicated to St. James, the miners' patron, could be started. It is a short structure of two bays, with a five-sided apsidal termination, which already since the beginning did not reckon with a triumphal arch, forming a single spatial unity with the triple nave. The comparatively shallow vaulting has no rising tendency; rather it is spread horizontally, as it was required by the conception of an aisled hall which should be attached to the choir. From the point of style we may distinguish two types of sculptured forms: those persisting from the stylistic supply of forms of the thirteenth century, now in fact obsolete, and the new ones which raise architectural work above the level of conventional building operations. To the former belong buttressing piers and window traceries, that is, forms determining the exterior aspect of style.

On the other hand, all forms beloging to the interior are completely new. The vaulting itself is of an unusal type: apart from large bosses placed at the crossing of diagonal ribs there are also smaller bosses at the apices whereby the tectonic system of vaulting compartments is rather confused. The central vaulting compartment is accentuated by a circular disk inserted beneath the vaulting ribs at their intersection. Its tectonic function is problematic; in reality it should represent a second boss emphasizing the wall at the expense of vaulting ribs. The same depreciating effect of tectonic forms may be traced in the engaged shafts. All of the three ribs of the vault meet upon a short corbel of concave shape, which simultaneously forms a cap of the shaft. Only under the central rib a simple rounded bar runs down to the ground. There is, however, something more belonging to the shaft: it is a wide piece of wall underlying it and reaching down to the window-sill, lined on either side with slender bars, which under the vault pass into mid-wall ribs. Ribs of this type could easily be employed in any kind of vault stressing its tectonic character; so far they have met upon the same corbel together with the rest of free vaulting ribs. At Kuttenberg they miss their corbel for the first time, forming a slightly projecting strip underlying the actual shaft. The reason for such an arrangement can be easily provided; in place of a sculptured form as represented by the tripartite shaft of High Gothic, another form is treated here determined by that portion of flat wall. And so the shaft of the choir at Kuttenberg belongs rather to the wall than to the vault, or rather to the surface of the wall than to the wall itself: it is a mere border attached to its surface.

St. James choir is not the only one illustrating the beginnings of Czech Gothic architecture: if it was not the same workshop it was at least some master closely related to it who constructed the nave together with the western part of the choir of St. Anne's Church in Prague. The present church was founded in about 1313 and in 1334, when it was remembered in the last will of a rich Prague burgher Konrád of Litoměřice, it had not yet been completed.

The vaulting supports of all six western bays resemble those of the Kuttenberg choir. Here, too, the free vaulting ribs rest upon a single corbel, carved in a similar manner as that of Kuttenberg and the mid-wall ribs also form a flat strip to which the actual shaft is then attached. The simple corbel of St. Anne's was treated in a similar way as the shaft at Kuttenberg: its connection with the core of the wall was spoilt by that slightly projecting insertion belonging to the wall and accentuating its two-dimensional character. The above mentioned burgher Konrád of Litoměřice, in his last will, also remembered the Chapel attached to the Minorite Church of St. James in the Old Town of Prague, that was built by his order before 1334. Its vaulting arranged in a square is supported by a central pillar. The vaulting ribs bond freely into its body, disappearing under its surface or resting upon a horizontal string-course. The tectonic inconsequence of such an arrangement is striking: the principle upon which the complex vaulting system is based fails just in the central support where it should be especially manifest and so the support being tectonically ineffective tells us nothing about the vaulting and the number of its ribs.

The round body of this pillar belongs, therefore, not to the vaulting and its ribs but to the wall, that is to say to its surface, optically enclosing the interior room of the chapel, which having returned back to itself found its optic centre in the pillar. In a similar way the people of this period returned back to their earthly existence from the mystical exaltations of religious imagination.

Since the very beginning of Czech Gothic architecture we can trace two artistic trends, following along much the same lines and attaining similar ends; the first, modelling the wall is apparent at Kuttenberg, while the second pervades St. James's in Prague and is concerned with the artistic purpose of interior room. Both these separate movements, however, meet before long to increase their effects. This happened for the first time, circa 1340, in the Chapter-Hall of a Benedictine Monastery situated on the river Sázava, which borrowed many stylistic elements in operation from the vestry and Chapter-Hall of the Augustinian Monastery at Roudnice; for example the caps of shafts, covered with horizontal mouldings or caps provided with a trefoiled tracery. The stiff plastic detail of animal figures is also reminiscent of Roudnice and it seems as if its natural movement was enchanted by the touch of a magic wand obeing some higher order than that of a natural living organism. It was employed on the central pillar within the Chapter-Hall of Sázava. We may, therefore, say that all the stiff and conventional forms found at Sázava are attributable to the influence of Roudnice. The proper sense of these forms, however, is to be sought somewhere else. It is no doubt that Roudnice supplied fundamental forms, yet their composition based on the style of the choirs at Kutná Hora and St. Anne's in Prague is completely new.

Let us observe the engaged shaft of Sázava, which recalls to us that of the choir at Kutná Hora. The shaft runs down a broad projecting band, framed by a wall rib, which is carried down to the ground and there it ends in slender cones. The proper shaft is provided with a cap, either circular and of horizontal moulding, or polygonal, curved with tracery, both being extremely big-headed. It is ended above the ground in a tiny cone so that it exercises the effect of a suspended, rather than a rising and supporting shaft.

The central pillar was formed in a very interesting way. It consisted of a cylindrical body into which the vaulting ribs bond quite freely, without any caps or mouldings, that is to say completely untectonically. The individual bars of the ribs are slightly detached from the pillar so that at least their outmost parts remain unabsorbed by it as in St. James's Vestry in Prague. Here, at Sázava, however, these parts do not end in a common portion of a horizontal moulding but each of them rests separately on a tiny shaft provided with a cap of horizontal moulding which runs along the surface of the pillar down to its base. It should obviously recall the classic form, known e. g. from the pillar within the crypt at Kouřim (about 1260—70), but the separate bars of the shafts are so subtle and so widely spaced that the cylindrical core of the pillar breaks through them upon the surface. Individual animal figures placed freely on the bodies of the shafts suggest that the original capitals of Roudnice were covered with sculptured figures.

It is obvious that the wall and the vaulting became distinct formations. We may also prove it by another fact. The Chapter-Hall is placed at a lower level than the floor of the adjacent cloister so that once it was connected with the cloister by a rather high staircase. In order to preserve the usual symmetrical arrangement of the doors and windows in the common wall it occurred that the central door, lying between the windows, found itself so high in the wall that there was no space left for the central vaulting corbel. Rather than spoil the optic symmetry of the wall, they preferred to break away with the quadripartite vault. In place of a single, central corbel on the west wall of the hall there were two on either side of the door. As there happened to be an opening opposite the pillar, the two western compartments of the vaulting were split into three, the central one assuming the form of a triangle. However spontaneous, this is, no doubt, the beginning of a stellar vault. It is very interesting for the future development of Czech Gothic architecture, as it is not the vault itself that gives impetus to the alternation of the cross-vault but the wall, or rather the disposition of its apertures. Until then the arrangement of the apertures in the wall depended on the vaults, but now it is the contrary. From this insignificant circumstance we may judge that the vaulting was treated only as an interpolation subordinated to the interior room and its walls.

The beginnings of Czech Gothic architecture may also be traced within the nave of the Franciscan Church at Plzeň, belonging to the second quarter of the fourteenth century. Its choir, triumphal arch and the eastern front of the aisles were constructed in about 1300. The exterior walls of the triple nave were erected during the first quarter of the subsequent century, while the nave walls with the arcades were completed in about 1340. The fabric was vaulted about the middle of the century. The manner in which the arches join their piers is very exceptional. Instead of robust early Gothic square piers we find here smooth cylindrical bodies without caps or mouldings wherein the arches simply end. This form corresponds in no way to tectonic order, and suggests a late Gothic principle.

In Austria the development of Gothic style followed along much the same lines as in Bohemia, only its optic and contra-tectonic tendencies are not so clearly expressed. Apart from the Monastery at Retz, two chapels are of importance here, attached to the large Mendicant Monasteries: St. George's Chapel at the Augustinian Monastery in Vienna (1327—41) and

St. John's Chapel. They were built by order of the lords of Wallsee, well known in Bohemia because of their marriage ties to the Vítkovci of Hradec. Both these buildings were erected by the self-same architectural school, as is obvious, not only from their double nave ground-plans but also from the forms of central piers. Similarly as in the Chapter-Hall at Sázava, here the piers have their own core, this time octagonal, in which the vaulting ribs end quite simply allowing their external parts to run down in the form of tiny shafts equipped with tiny caps and bases.

If we survey the first phase of Gothic style it is necessary to emphasize its negative work at first, viz., its striving after reduction whereby it suppressed the tectonic form (the Franciscan Church of Plzeň), its tendency to neutralize the tectonic form (the central pillar at St. James's in Prague) and its attemps to spoil the tectonic function of members obtained from the older stylistic supply (the hanging canopy in the Chapter-Hall at Sázava). Its positive effort was directed to the transformation of massive wall into an immaterial cover, changing sculptured forms into flat, unexpressive members (the shafts at Kutná Hora, at St. Anne's in Prague and at Sázava) and trying to impart optic qualities upon them. Thus it produced interior rooms independent of the vaulting system in which the vaults were treated only as subordinate insertions predetermined by the disposition of walls and their openings. In this way the style created the first stellar vaults that were essentially different from those of England and Germany, as they are not formed by multiplying the rib but result from the alternate displacement of vaulting supports.

The tragic end of the battle of Crécy in August 26th, 1346, suddenly completed what had been slowly in preparation in Bohemia for several years. John of Luxemburg, a foreigner in his Bohemian Kingdom, was succeeded by his son, Margrave Charles, who, French by education but Czech on his mother's side, had sojourned in Bohemia since 1333, governing its affairs as a provincial administrator. He was elected King of the Holy Roman Empire only one and a half months before that unhappy battle took place and from 1347 he wore the crown of the Bohemian Kingdom.

Bohemia soon stood at the head of German Empire, passing it in the race during a few years, which may be illustrated by some important historical dates. As early as 1344, Charles established the Archbishopric in Prague thus making Bohemia independent of the German ecclesiastical organisation and in the same year he founded St. Vitus Cathedral. From 1347 the new Archbishop possessed the right of crowning the King of Bohemia. In 1348 Prague was enlarged by the New Town so that it grew substantially in population and area and the University which was then founded, gave Bohemia cultural independence as well. At the same time, political relationships were established with Silesia and Upper Lusatia and they were declared direct fiefs of the Bohemian Crown. In 1355 an attempt was made to establish a general imperial law and a year afterwards the Golden Bull regulated the relations of the Bohemian King towards the Holy Roman Empire and awarded him preference amongst the Imperial Electors. Every moment of Charles' rich life from the first years of his French sojourn up to his last journey to France seems to have brought enormous profit to Bohemia in every respect; political, ecclesiastical and cultural.

Hand in hand with political prosperity there seemed to be the necessity to represent the power of state partly by the dynasty and person of the sovereign, according to medieval custom. For this reason a picture gallery was placed in the anteroom of the King's Palace comprising portraits of all Charles' predecessors upon the Roman throne, including sovereigns of ancient Rome while the shrine of Charlemagne was preserved in the newly founded Karlov Church. Czech national pride was further strengthened by the fact that Emperor Charles based his political power upon local historical tradition, restoring ancient ties that bound him to the extinct Premyslides whose descendent Charles felt himself to be. This is apparent from a new order succession to the Bohemian throne establishing the coronation ceremony upon the legendary tradition of Vyšehrad (the oldest castle in Prague) and consecrating the Crown of Bohemia together with the Prague Castle to St. Wenceslas. There are many other examples available of similar honours; the rebuilding of Vyšehrad Castle and Curch, as well as its fortifications, and incorporation in the ground-plan of the town, Charles' care of Stadice and its princely hazel-bush or the dignified deposition of the tombs of several Premyslides within the chapels of St. Vitus Cathedral. Emperor Charles also attempted to embellish Bohemia and its capital, mainly by many shrines or rather curiosities. This was quite natural and peculiar to the time, as we learn, for instance, from the medieval books of travel which make it apparent how higly such things were appreciated then and what spiritual value was generally ascribed to them.

Large structures and sculpture, of course, found their due place and use in the political tendencies of the time. We need not think only of the Prague Cathedral, which being a real manifestation of political power and independence of church organisation, grew into an enormous architecture dominating Prague. It is sufficient to point out its ideological significance, as represented by the Chapel and tomb of St. Wenceslas, whose name became a symbol of the very essence of typical Czech features; or observe how, above the gallery of the Premyslides a second gallery grew in the triforium within the cathedral representing contemporary Czech hierarchy — secular and ecclesiastical — from the Emperor down to the architect of the building; above the second gallery there is a third gallery of Bohemian patron saints and we can realize the importance of the task assigned to the co-operation of the artist in this work. We may also remember the purpose of other building enterprises of Emperor Charles — the Karlštejn Castle with its pictorial enrichment as well as the Old Town Tower erected on the road to the Royal Castle which, on approach suddenly appears to the astonished spectator in its full outline, and we can realise the power of the idea of State which pervaded all the sculptured details of its façade. Also evident are the robust coats of arms bearing heraldic devices of the individual lands of the Bohemian Kingdom, among which the emblems of Bohemia and Moravia were distinguished from others by rich jewels, as well as by their outstanding positions.

It is natural that art, thus engaged in political ideas should develop quicker than it did formerly in the bourgeois milieu. In towns, too, this progress became apparent in the increased number of newly built architecture. In the New Town of Prague the churches of St. Giles and St. James were in the course of completion and Týn, St. Michael, St. Castulus, St. Gallus and the Church of the Holy Ghost were being erected, as well as the Tower of the Charles Bridge and that of the City Town Hall. In the Lesser Town, St. Thomas was being completed and the Church of St. John's Knights was under reconstruction. All these enterprises were carried out by rich burghers.

The New Town, on the other hand, was founded by Emperor Charles, who himself introduced building regulations, measured up the streets and secured a twelve years'exemption from taxes. There is no wonder that new churches sprang up here so quickly that they surprise us even now-a-days by their artistic uniformity and purity of style. The foundation stone of the New Town of Prague was laid on the 26th of March 1348 and by 1350 it already was surrounded by exterior fortifications. We know that in 1351 there were two parochial churches, St. Henry and St. Stephan, and some monastic churches as well, pertaining to new monastic orders in which all the richness of the spiritual life of that time became manifest. Thus arose, in the year 1348, the Benedictine Monastery of Emmaus, na Slovanech, with services in the old Slavonic tongue, in 1350 (e. i. one year after the coronation of Charles at Aachen) Karlov Church, in 1355 (one year after his coronation at Milan) the Church of the Benedictines of St. Ambrose Order, and the Augustinian Nunnery of St. Katherine, as well as the Monastery of the Virgin Mary na Trávníčku (1360) and the Church of St. Apollinaris na Větrově (1362). In addition the Monastic Church of the Virgin Mary-in-the-Snow of the Carmelite Order was founded one year before the rise of the New Town. Nine large churches on the whole were thus started nearly simultaneously and constructed so quickly that no other church throughout Bohemia could rival them. It is a matter of fact that Emperor Charles was concerned with their constructions, and some of these buildings originated because of his intimate wishes and the personal experiences he gained during his journeys abroad. A great number of older buildings were obliged to give way to the new art of building which unheedingly enforced the right of its own expression. Sometimes, even time-honoured monuments reaching back to the very threshold of our national history were demolished, for instance Spytihněv's Basilica of St. Vitus together with its cloister, comprising the relics of St. Wenceslas Rotunda; or the old Court Chapel of the Premyslides attached to the Royal Palace; St. Peter's Church at Vyšehrad, St. Martin-in-the-Wall, St. Castulus, St. Gallus, St. Peter, the Church of Týn Hospital, St. Mary of the Knights of St. John and a chapel which used to stand in the place of St. Apollinaris Church. In the Middle Ages a new and more majestic building could fully recompense the value even of the oldest monuments, for spiritual content prevailed at that time and though wholly reconstructed, the church remained the self-same building in the minds of the people by then.

These are but the external features of the turning-point in Czech history which occurred after the succession of Emperor Charles to the throne of Bohemia. Much more essential and important for the history of Czech art was the change of spiritual environment, in preparation, from the date of Charles'return from France (1333). Its character, so far as it concerned the medieval conception of the world, remained essentially unaltered, even in the latter part of the fourteenth century. In spite of the suggestions of awakening scepticism, evident for instance, in the early works of Parler, culture continued to be governed by spiritualism enclosing life within the acts of Creation and Redemption, while history remained a struggle between God and the Devil, and nature a stage full of miracles. Incessant intrigues of evil powers compelled man to be cautious in temporary things. However, the psychological basis of spiritual life of the contemporary society was considerably changed, which is obvious from the fact that the standard-bearer of spiritual life was no longer the medieval knight as was still the case under King John, but a man of learning educated by the university who became, at least formally, acquainted with classical literature. It was not by chance alone that the most distinguished men of the time, graduates of the leading universities (foreign, of course, at first), were simultaneously active men of letters and that the first private libraries originated, at that period, even among the bourgeoisie. Czech life rejected its former aloofness opening up the way to European ideological currents. Due to the influence exerted by the court, French culture, above all, found favour in Bohemia; both the southern sensual from the environment of the Pope's Holy See at Avignon and the northern speculative from the territory around Paris. The King himself once spent seven of his youthful years in France and the bishop of Dražice, eleven and the first queen — Beatrix, was French by birth and spirit. It is generally known that French intellectualism penetrated the very personality of Charles whose literary works, mostly autobiographical, historical, legal and religious, rank him among the foremost writers of that period and who, influenced by Italian Humanism, was in contact with Petrarch, its Florentine founder. For our purpose, however, it is necessary to emphazise Charles' initiative not only in the sphere of literary and historical works but especially in works of art. We meet with it in Karlštejn Castle, St. Vitus Cathedral and the Court Chapel at Prague Castle, as well as in the selection of churches and their types in the New Town. His knowledge of art and its problems was not manifest in mere maecenatism which still prevailed in John IV. of Dražice. He proceeded methodically and consciously to exert influence, not only upon fundamental architectural conceptions (in St. Vitus, All Saints' Chapel, at Karlštejn and in Karlov Church), but also upon the selection of artists and forms of style. How keenly he could distinguish the individual trends and how quickly he recognized the momentary Czech needs is obvious from the fact that none of his new buildings belonged to the Danubian linear style arising out of the atmosphere of German mysticism. He selected builders from countries of which the spiritual structure was closely related to Czech character. The first court architect, Mathias of Arras, came directly from Avignon to found his cathedral in a style whose abstract linearism was already spoilt by southern sensualism, while the second builder, Peter Parler, related Czech art again to the artistic atmosphere of Swabia which, as we have pointed out, already competed with Bohemia in the preceding period.

The increasing spiritual sensualism manifested itself in Czech cultural life immediately from the beginning in two ways: partly by its strong individualistic character and partly in that man of that time started to be interested in his earthly existence. The spirit of this new man of learning began to tend directly to the reality of the mundane world which in art soon became evident in so many different trends that it seems as though some long forgotten classical forms were then revided. Signs of maecenatism are already apparent in the works of John of Dražice and Charles in a manner that can rightly be denoted as early Humanism. At that period the first attempts were being made towards an understanding of human existence. In literature we meet with biographies and autobiographies wherein, in spite of their purely spiritualistic character, we can trace some portraying features. In painting and sculpture there suddenly appears an enormous need for portraits and auto-portraits, witnessing the increased interest in personal appearance which, however, are often subservient to the idea of State (the portraits of Charles IV in St. Vitus Gallery, at the Prague Castle and at Tangermünde, in the mural paintings of Karlštejn, on shrines, votive tablets and others). The reverence for creative genius unknown until then, now found its due place in life. It was based on subjective esteem, therefore, the names of the artists began to appear in connection with their works while the artists themselves played important roles in society (the busts of both builders of St. Vitus Cathedral were placed in the suite of secular hierarchy in the triforium).

This change may also be traced in man's effort to leave some souvenir of himself so as not to die in the memory of future generations. It is to this effort that art owes many a stimulating impulse. Thus, John IV of Dražice was concerned lest his name be forgotten. He, therefore, provided all his works with coats of arms bearing his heraldic devices and had a chronicler describe his fruitful life. For the same reason he placed memorial plates on his buildings giving an account of their foundation, building progress and his own share in them, which later became the rule with Parler's buildings (triforium inscriptions, the plate on St. Vitus Cathedral or in the choir at Kolín). Similarly, the names of all Charles' foundations such as Karlsberg, Karlsfried, Karlshaus, Karlskrone, Karlstein and Karlsburg testify to this effort (however under the influence of the fashion to Germanize) to preserve one's own name and memory. The individual man suddenly rises above the level of collective convention, striving after an artistic creation of his own. The sense of the originality of creation and form began to be manifest in art, particularly when its individual categories were freed from their old dependence on architecture and when panel painting and free sculpture, both taking up their own space, began to replace fresco and architectural sculpture. Man simply started to manage things after his own desire in this temporal earthly environment. In philosophico-religious questions and in art this new sensualistic basis brought forth a new way of thinking and creating. It is natural that in an age whose character was as transitory as that of Charles a uniform philosophical conception or a unique style in art can hardly be taken into consideration. The old spiritual trends have survived here side by side, for a long time bound to older generations or — which occured more frequently — to certain social groups, as for instance, the monasteries. Therefore, we may distinguish at that period three main spiritual and stylistic currents in architecture running parallel: the northern French form of a classical cathedral brought to Bohemia by Peter Parler from Cologne on the Rhine and representing, of course, not without reserve, objective French rationalism, still able to bear the pathos of the idea of State, next to the linear Danubian style pervading monastic and municipal buildings and following along much the same lines as the subjective expressiveness of German mysticism of the first quarter of the cenutry — and lastly there is the actual Czech trend of a sensual character which, when compared to the German trend shows a secularizing tendency, and as against the French it tends to individualism. This is also why no unifying conception can be attained in the questions of faith and religion. We meet here especially with the expiring but not yet extinct speculative spiritualism whereby the Dominicans enlivened some of the fundamental themes of scholasticism of which the sparks every now and then burst into flame upon the official University ground in order to become actualized at a later period in the theory of Hussitism. In addition, there is the German mysticism surviving in mendicant monasteries as late as the close of the century, giving up direct rational control, and attempting to transform the abstract scholastic theories into sensual experiences. A "direct vision" of God and Saints is then brought, in a popular form, into the suburbs of towns where from time immemorial the Mendicants had settled in order to evoke social undercurrents among the common people which were often transferred to the field of social ethics or practical morality in general. Moreover, we find here also the doctrine of the younger Franciscan school, manifesting the post-classical, i. e. the post-theoretic scepticism represented by the names of Duns Scotus (1266 —1308, W. Occam (1270—1374), and his successor Nicolas d'Autrecourt (died after 1350), who as against the certainty of Dominican intellectualism and scholastic speculation on creed, emphasize the essence of Christian learning, thus returning to the Bible as the only source of faith. They consider faith to be an act of love and will rather than a question of rationalistic recognition of God and similarly they prefer morality to every sort of speculation. This state is very typical of the end of classical rationalism in religion, which in the field of philosophy appears as the victory of nominalism over realism, of sensual understanding over speculation and which necessitates ascribing real existence only to sensually perceived phenomena while abstract ideas and conceptions should be referred to unreality. The confidence in sensual experience and a-priority of the realm of sensual experience led, in the middle of the fourteenth century, to a separation of creed and science and to the slow rise of natural sciences. We still do not know exactly whether and with what understanding the Czech intelligentsia of the time took part in this spiritual struggle of which the meeting ground was Paris and Oxford, for the Prague University, most probably, had a reactionary standpoint in some respects. This new spirit manifested itself in Bohemia, spontaneously at least, in the so-called "devotio moderna", i. e. piety penetrated by modern humanistic and aesthetic elements. It was professed by a new Order of the Canons of St. Augustine who in their programme returned to their patron saint whose spirit comprised both the ancient and medieval worlds, thus simultaneously expressing opposition against the speculative Aristotelian basis of scholastic trends. The sensualism of the Augustinian spiritual movement arose directly in Italy, its cradle being Pavia; it was introduced into Bohemia by the bishop John of Dražice from southern France in the year 1333, in spite of the resistance of German Mendicant Orders. This new trend appeared to be so related to the Czech spirit that it soon gained the favour of the Court as well as that of the first Archbishop and the Augustinians became the leading monastic order of Bohemia. Their unascetic devotion brought abstract and earthly things together and their emphasis on civilization and aestheticism of religious ideas also made their artistic sensual experience subservient to faith and they celebrated God's name by sensually beautiful works. All this brought about great stimulus to the development of creative art and music as well, so that the Church opened up the way to late Gothic style in Bohemia immediately at its outset. People thus obtained everything that in the ecclesiastical art of the latter half of the fourteenth century tended to sensual life and through it directly to human sensibility. It is especially the devout reverence for the Virgin Mary, symbol of eternal womanhood, that found expression in Bohemia towards the end of the century in the gracious and sensually sweet figures of madonnas, next to a number of legendary elements fully understood in their original lifelikeness illustrating a really human struggle of a saint. We can well imagine how near all this was to a simple Czech man and how it enabled the common people to take part in meditations on religious doctrines as it did not call for previous theoretic education, giving rise to an intense interest in spiritual questions and thus preparing the ground for the popular undercurrent in the Hussite revolution.

Similarly in art, sensualism appeared as a result of an increased certainty in the external, that is, sensual knowledge. This, of course, became most apparent in those branches of creative arts wherein the relation towards sensual reality plays the most important part, namely in painting and sculpture. Only by rejecting abstraction, illustrative character and subordination to the realm of conceptions were these arts given the possibility of free development and in this way they also found artistic purpose of their own. Painting being the most sensual means of artistic expression was first of all stimulated by a mightly impulse so that it quickly excelled architecture itself, which, after all, deals with far more abstract forms and placed itself at the head of a contemporary stylistic movement. This new sensual relation towards the outward world, which Czech painting took up, was enabled, firts of all, to grasp all the hitherto-existing results of sensual Italian painting: so that during the first phase of its development (about 1340—60) it became acquainted with the Italian objective manner of depicting space by means of complex architectures and with the southern conception of plastically modelled sculptured forms as well as with the emphasis on colour and colourfulness typical of every kind of sensualism. Although painting retained its northern abstract character in Bohemia, its colourfulness assumed an optical tendency apt to model form which had till then been done only by means of a monochromatic plane and line. Sensual experience, however, once awakened in Czech man made him dissatisfied with a simple adoption of the Italian school of painting. His activity could not be limited to the sharp realistic note accompanying Italian painting which causes space as well as form to be treated by objective means. And so as early as the period of 1360—80, remarkable attemps were being made in Bohemia to start one's own school of painting expressing itselft by a more sensual means which is so peculiar to subjective painting, that is by modelling in colour without contouring, and rejecting the Italian objective diversity of forms. This style distinguishing itself by intensity of colouring, soft forms and depth of tone, and accompanied by an enormous sensibility and surprising naturalism, was created in the middle of the Sixties by the Court painter Theodorich. It has no analogy in contemporary foreign countries and its relative maturity which hardly corresponds to the development of older Czech panel painting, still prevents art historians from definitely deciding whether it is a style of domestic origin. However, its tectonically relaxed forms governing not only the modelling of faces and hands but also transforming the drapery into bag-resembling formations, as well as its contra-Italian tendency, apparent in the indifference towards the tectonic construction of space, may only be explained as the extreme results of the same sensualism which, having rejected all reminiscences of older spiritual movements, also found its expression in contemporary Czech architecture.

From the same domestic source there arose shortly before 1380, the excellent art of a master painter emloyed by the Augustinians of Třeboň; in him Czech painting suddenly surpassed the entire environment of central Europe. The spiritualism whereby he solves his philosophico-religious attitude towards the outer world distinguishes him from the melancholic naturalism of Theodorich; he, however, excells Theodorich in conceiving the picture as a framed section of the actual world. The landscape, though still in a coulisse-like manner, reappears in painting, while depth is often given to space even for objects in perspective. The individual figures are grouped in a natural and lively whole and at the same time the first suggestions of perspective appear. In order to flood this proportional and spatial whole of the picture with a uniform light the artist elaborated a special chiaroscuro technique which causes the figures that are more important for the action and content to be more expressive by brighter illumination while subordinate things are suppressed by means of twilight as was the habit afterwards in Baroque painting. This was something completely new and unknown in Europe, a discovery, arising directly out of Czech sensual creativity which attained its climax by the Augustinian workshop. In the art of building it was the Church of Třeboň which analogously completed the development of Gothic style, showing us that the sources of this art were really of domestic origin and that it is not necessary to apply artificial explications of foreign influences to them.

Czech sculpture followed along uncertain lines at that time. Its development, split into several trends, was not as uniform as that of contemporary architecture. This lies already in its very character, as a sculpturer can better correct his optic perception by what he knows about the represented massive form. Even here, in the beginnings of a sensualistic transformation we meet with the endeavour to become acquainted with the results of Italian development based most probably on a similar effort of contemporary painting. However, Parler's school soon prevailed. Not being uniform in its style, it retained a mystical liking for slender expressive forms in addition to tendencies towards ponderous, tectonic and fully massive forms. And so only a few stone-carvers achieved the desired picturesque effect, as Opitz pointed out, manifesting itself in the predominance of concave forms over convex ones, in producing the effect of light and shade, and in the nichelike deepening of the background. For this reason also the idealistic and spiritualistic conception of a model alternates here, so frequently, with realistic attempts at portrait or genre painting which does not avoid even a grimace.

The beginnings of optic conception in so complicated a branch as that of town architecture were determined by many exterior components and may only be traced in the composition of the New Town of Prague. The hitherto-existing functional articulation of the town mass, based on the significance of a building and corresponding to the abstract classic basis, starts to be replaced by an optic composition laying stress on the dominating situation of a bulding, no longer because of its significance but because of the spectacle it presented. In the New Town it was all the more possible as it arose by order of a single person — the sovereign; to his uniform will we may also ascribe the dominating situation of the churches "na Slovanech", St. Apollinaris, "na Větrově", and of the Karlov Church which exercised a striking influence on the appearance of the town. The same optic composition is to be found in the inner reconstruction of St. Vitus Cathedral completed by the south tower and a portal so that for the future its optic relation towards the town should prevail over its tectonic logicality and symmetry of its interior ground-plan. All this witnesses the rise of a new conception in architecture based on the situation of a building.

It would take us long if we wanted to trace the results of this awakened sensualism in Gothic music or in literature; it is sufficient to point out that it emphasized the sensual, that is to say acoustic quality of tone and word achieving thus increased musicality of tone. In recitative music there appeared the necessity of musical rhythm while in folk music, choral songs came into being sung by two voices running parallel. Also in poetry the acoustic perception is more important than the meaning of the word so that it is often acoustic quality that determines the selection and arrangement of words. For this reason, for instance, in the Legend of St. Katherine the sound of the words is stressed while the separate verses are joined by alliteration.

All this new effort we have just followed in all branches of human creation differed from the previous movements in another way as well: while in every phase of rationalism the purpose of a work of art went before its sensually conceived form, in sensualism it is the very contrary; here, form goes before content. So it came about that apart from the transcendental world which was created by the Early Middle Ages as a superior world of spiritual values and bound to the theories of the classical period, there arises the world of form and aesthetic effect, experienced through the senses and judged by the deliciousness of a sensual feeling of beauty. This is already the world of modern art. The birth of modern man thus has its roots in the fourteenth century together with free artistic forms independent of ideas and religious content. The modern conception of beauty pervaded art: it penetrated written and oral expression giving rise to ornate style, while literature was changed into belles lettres; in the creative arts it affected the composition so that the artist began to be concerned with regularity, accuracy and formal accomplishment of form. The age-old functionality gave way to formalism which was soon afterwards changed into l'art pour l'art intellectualism of the clasess living in the centre of social life.

On account of all this emotional awakening of medieval man, northern abstract thinking was rejected and the individuality of the genuinely Czech personality gradually came into being. In this way that type of Czech sentimental patriotism originated which has persisted down to the present day, together with the national consciousness which pervaded the classes of noblemen and intelligentsia, manifesting itself throughout Czech cultural and political life. When in the year 1333 John of Dražice founded his Monastery at Roudnice he reserved it solely for Czech monks being aware of many a grivous moment when the intolerance of German monasticism troubled his life. The Czech element prevailed in the New Town of Prague from the beginning and penetrated soon afterwards into the walls of Germanism in the rest of the royal towns. The Czech language was introduced into high politics promoting the idea of State. Charles IV based even the policy of the Holy Roman Empire upon Czech cultural tradition, dynasty and statesmanship which found expression not only in the fact that he ideologically derived his political power as the King of Bohemia from the superior conception of the Bohemian Crown but also in that he raised the Czech language to the level of a political language, which soon pervaded public charters. He also expressed the desire that the sons of Electors should learn Czech and that Germans should honour the patron saints of Bohemia. There is no wonder that the new Augustinian Church at Lower Ingelsheim on the river Danube was dedicated to St. Wenceslas, which testifies to the effort of Emperor Charles, and it was colonised by native Czechs from Karlov in Prague. A general reverence for St. Wenceslas spread during his reign as far as Hamburg and over the rest of the Hanseatic towns. Thus the idea of Czech nationality and state rivals that of the German Empire in importance and monumentality which brought even Petrarch's reproach to Charles. In the Karlštejn Castle erected to preserve the Crown Jewels of the Empire we also meet with its suggestion in the form of a pictorial representation of the lives of St. Wenceslas and St. Ludmila, and we can even trace it in those of the German castles representing direct Bohemian fiefs, such as the newly founded Tangermünde in Brandenburg Mark, the main hall of which Charles had provided about 1374 with a fresco depicting himself among the Electors and containing also the figures of Bohemian sovereigns, dukes, kings, and queens from the earliest Premyslides down to youthful Václav. Emperor Charles also contributed to the spiritual emancipation of his nation: he founded the Archbishopric and University in Prague which soon met with practical results. The Czech language, becoming not only a means but the very object of cultural creative power, soon laid the foundation to a rich Czech literature while the Bohemianized towns introduced a Czech element into those social classes which had, until then, possessed the sole privilege of producing works of art. Since that time the Czechs have become prominent artists, founding families of builders, Czech names entered the lists of town-guilds and Czech stone-carvers appear in the city-councillor's bodies of towns. And so it occurred that since then we can speak of a genuinely Czech art because the Czech element took part in its further development with ever increasing effort so that under the King Wenceslas IV it governed not only the architecture of our towns but also the art of the Court.

Thus thanks to so noble a sovereign and patriot, the Czech nation stood at the head of the foremost nations of the Holy Roman Empire its importance grew and the process of Bohemianizing cultural life and work advanced; all this resulted in the Czechs reaching a point which, until then, had only been attained by the German nation. Bohemia was raised to play the leading part in the Danubian district, too, and placed itself at the head of its art.

In this way Emperor Charles also exerted influence upon the late Gothic art of Danubia whose Czech character is indisputable in its very beginnings.

THE PERIOD OF 1350—60

The decade of 1350—60 was inaugurated by two triple nave churches: St. Nicolas (now known as Giles) at Nymburk and St. Stephen in the New Town of Prague. Both of them belong to the new type of a post-classical basilican church for their naves are provided with external buttresses which pierce through the vaulting of the aisles and penetrate into their spaces. Both churches show a common effort to shorten the length of the triple nave as much as possible while it was simultaneously widened in its scope. At Nymburk the nave comprises only 4 × 3 vaulting compartments, like that in Prague, where the tower was already included within the nave space, whereas at Nymburk there are two flanking towers placed before the nave. We notice that this period is concerned with the interior room, calmly resting and uniformly extended throughout the triple nave; it was no longer expressively overemphasized but freed itself from its dependence upon the altar of the choir. The triple nave, so unnaturally lengthened in the first part of the century, assumed again its natural proportions and having rejected the expressive and mystical tendency returned back to itself.

This escape from mystical expressiveness of the first half of the fourteenth century, so characteristic of Czech spirit, has brought about a change in the exterior aspect of a building, too. While at Nymburk the massive towers appear to rise directly from the ground forming an obstruction to a free extension of the nave gable which is squeezed in between them, the towers of St. Stephen's in Prague show quite a different tendency. We learn from the original designs that but one south tower should be erected here. This should add to the picturesque effect of the church. Its outline has thus changed according to the point whence it was observed. Optic regards, prevalent here, testify that the external aspect of the building has passed through a Bohemianizing process as well.

So far as the sculptured details of these buildings are concerned, we do not find here, for the first time, either caps or corbels which have till then expressed and emphasized the tectonic function of ribs. The vaulting shafts die simply into the wall. The form and manner whereby the vault meets the wall was thus altered and similarly the formerly massive wall was changed into a flat and immaterial structure upon which the vaulting rested flatly and weightlessly, too, without the assistance of the massive core of the wall. The same striving after uniformity and simplification may be traced in the development of aisled halls. There are three large hall churches belonging to this period: St. Henry, the Church of the Virgin Mary in Prague and Frauenkirche at Nuremberg; each of them is of a different origin.

Towards the close of the first part of the fourteenth century Bohemia could follow but a single model of an aisled hall which had just been created in Central Germany, combining the classical hall as represented first of all by St. Elizabeth at Marburg with that of Westphalia based on the cathedral at Poitiers. The result was a triple nave of equal width, completely absorbing the transept which formerly divided the nave from the choir. Even if the aisled halls of German type were of equal height and often also of equal width, they retained an exaggerated elongation in the direction of the altar whereby their ground-plans were considerably deformed, and just in this point the development of Czech style started to liberate the triple nave — similarly as was the case already with the basilicae — from its dependence upon the choir and the altar, creating an interior of natural proportions, built upon an approximately square ground-plan. For this reason, each of these Czech halls of that time seems to be short compared to German ones. It is, namely, of equal width and length so that one could freely pass through it in all directions. In order to attain this aim it was necessary to shorten the vaulting compartments to 3×3 and, so far as the fabric is concerned, everything that spoilt the uniformity of the interior should be removed — first of all the arcades, dividing the nave from the aisles, were replaced by simple ribs. The final aim of the building shell was to attain a formation to which the choir could be attached by its flank without having affected any further change therein. With it is also connected the question of the form of central pillars which, forming central points of the interior, should no longer be directed towards the altar.

St. Henry's Church in Prague was founded by order of Emperor Charles in 1348. It has a choir of 3 bays and a triple nave of 4×3 vaulting compartments. The tower is included within the southern square of the triple nave, opening out into it in order not to spoil its uniformity. Although a longitudinal tendency prevails in the ground-plan, the formerly vertical character of the interior is gone, as the triple nave is at least twice as wide as it is high.

So far as the interior room is concerned, the Church of the Virgin Mary proceeded somewhat further towards the final aim of a Czech aisled hall. Founded by Emperor Charles, it was built in the years 1355—61; the choir of 3 vaulting compartments is attached to a triple nave of 3×3 vaulting squares; it is a completely square and symmetrical formation wherein both the main axes are perfectly balanced; however, more important is the fact that the widely spanned arches were replaced throughout the building by only slightly reinforced vaulting ribs. The pillars, four in number, stand freely in the church, with their cylindrical bodies resembling those of the Chapel at St. James in Prague. The development of space has been realized here in a surprisingly new and uncompromising manner.

The Augustinian Church of the Virgin Mary na Karlově in the New Town of Prague belongs here on account of its interior arrangement, though its choir was not completed until a much later date while the nave remained in an unfinished state during the whole period of the Hussite revolution. The Augustinian Order was founded by Charles IV in 1350 and as early as 1351 the construction was commenced. As the relics of Charlemagne obtained directly from Aachen on the occasion of the Emperor's coronation it should be preserved within the church, and it should recall in content, as well as in form, that of Aachen built in the form of a great octagon at the end of the eighth and beginning of the ninth century on the model of Ravenna church. For this reason an octagonal nave should be added to an oblong choir, consecrated in 1377. As we have already noticed such a development corresponded to that of the aisled hall, so that in spite of its foreign origin the design of Emperor Charles was neither alien nor contradictory to Czech art. Its unarticulated interior lying under the present Renaissance cupola, built as late as 1575, was of course contradictory to Czech art of the XIVth century. The architect of the XIVth century would certainly miss central supports and vaulting compartments of which the articulation and position resulted from the proportions of the triumphal arch. We may, therefore, suppose that its nave should originally have four cylindrical columns (—perhaps like that at Nuremberg) from which the ribs radiated so that the case was an aisled hall of 3×3 vaulting compartments.

The Czech character of a centrally designed aisled hall whose beginnings we have just followed can best be shown when we compare it to the German type, designed on a basilican plan with its interior subordinated to the altar. The aisles formed but narrow passages forcibly elongated, each of them terminating in a polygonal choir of its own. In order to preserve this fundamental disposition even after the transformation into an aisled hall it was necessary to retain the ground-plan of the aisles, the robust nave arcades, as well as the piers designed with regard to the altar. Triumphal arches, on the other hand, could be rejected so that polygonal choirs and the aisled hall were now of equal height. This type of an aisled hall has developed since the beginning of the fourteenth century in the Danubian district based on the elongated triple nave of Burgundian churches which provided the model for Ratisbon Cathedral. Thus the choir of St. Stephen in Vienna constructed as early as 1304—40, could combine the Burgundian post-classical design of a three-choir ground-plan with an aisled hall of equal height with these choirs.

The Monastery of Emmaus na Slovanech, founded in the New Town of Prague by Emperor Charles in 1347, belongs to this type of Austrian hall. Its foundation was preceded by negotiations between Charles and the Pope at Avignon in 1346. The result was that the Benedictine monks were allowed to say mass in the old Slavonic language; the church was dedicated to the Virgin Mary and St. Jerome (who was believed to be of Slavonic origin) next to the patron saints of the Bohemian Kingdom, St. Constantine, Methodius, Adalbert and Prokop. In 1348 this new order was established and simultaneously the building operations began. This marvellous masterpiece of Czech Gothic was at last consecrated in 1372 by the Archbishop John.

If we survey the period of 1350—60, we see that it especially brought about new types of aisled halls and basilicae. While the previous period was concerned with tectonic members of style, namely, with vaulting supports, the early times of Charles created a new conception of interiors, modelling the plain mass of the wall. However, based on older tradition, it achieved independent results giving rise to a new type of church. It attempted a new composition of mass and space and so it came about that this independent conception of a church and its form which arose in Bohemia, can be found nowhere else throughout Europe, thus expressing the artistic genius of the Czech nation as well as a genuine Czech manner of conceiving fundamental structural elements of architecture. If we want to learn the part that Emperor Charles took in this creative process, it is sufficient to call to mind that he stood at the cradle of each of the discussed churches, fully aware of the artistic purpose of Czech creative struggle immediately since its beginning.

THE PERIOD OF 1360—70

After 1360 Emperor Charles did not take part in the building operations as frequently as in the previous years, for now most of the parochial or monastic churches were built in country towns, and all were bourgeois enterprises. The majority of them sprang up in the provinces, although Prague retained its leading position insofar as the new types of buildings were concerned; we may, therefore, meet with some obsolete features in the countryside, which would hardly occur in Prague itself.

Only two of the monastic churches of our country towns were built to a basilican plan: one belonging to the Augustinian Order at Litomyšl, the other to the Dominicans of Budějovice. Both of them are bound by older tradition; that of Litomyšl follows the example of the Roudnice Church and that at Budějovice is modelled on the post-classical basilica of the Dominican Order.

It is obvious that obsolete types of these buildings are due to former practice of the respective orders; otherwise aisled halls prevailed throughout the country towns. It is, however, interesting to observe that it has not always been the centrally conceived hall of Czech type, as exemplified by the parochial churches at Kuttenberg and that of St. James and of the Virgin Mary na Náměti, that were erected in the third quarter of the fourteenth century. Their lofty interiors, evoking the impression of mystical solemnity, were strikingly elongated which, however, prevented them from attaining the final aim of Czech style. The symmetrical twin tower façade was finally rejected in both of the churches. In the Church of the Virgin Mary there is but one central tower similarly at St. Stephen in Prague, whereas in St. James only the townward tower was erected while the south tower, transformed into a low polygon, was then altogether abandoned. With this arrangement the regularity and longitudinal tendency of the exterior aspect of these churches were spoilt, giving way to a picturesque, centrally enclosed formation as was the case in Prague during the previous decade.

Because the building effort of the provinces had to gain upon that of Prague first, there is no wonder that new types will solely be found in Prague. It is again Emperor Charles who founded many churches here, for example St. Peter and Paul's Church at Vyšehrad. Its erection was included in a general reconstruction of this time-honoured princely seat, for the old collegiate church had already been in a ruinous state. It was not until the end of the fourteenth century that the building was completed. Four oblong chapels are attached here to the aisles, placed between the buttresses on the exterior of the building. Being of equal height and width with the aisles, these chapels were included within the exterior walls of the triple nave. There were no arcades dividing them from the aisles, so that their vaults meet in a common simple rib. The chapels were most probably modelled on those of St. Vitus Cathedral which should line its sides after the example of large cathedrals of Southern France.

The artistic value of such a conception was remarkable; thanks to this skilful treatment this type of basilica gained new impetus and a similar revival may be traced in Gothic art of Bavaria and Austria at the beginning of the XVth century.

The period of 1360—70 witness an entirely uncommon and surprising type of church created in Prague. It consisted of a double nave provided with a row of pillars. This formation prevailed in the majority of late Gothic churches in Austria and the adjacent Southern Bohemia. How fruitful the art of Prague was by then may also be seen by the fact that the new double nave came into being in two forms, each corresponding to one of the fundamental tendencies of the period: in the form of a centrally planned church following the example of Czech parochial "hall" churches and in the form of a longitudinal church which should better correspond to the conception of a monastic church with its subordination to the altar. Both formations are, however, variations of the self-same fundamental theme, attempting to fulfil a similar task whereby the entire contemporaneous effort of Czech Gothic art was occupied, namely to create interior room free of mysticism and imaginary relativity, which would be pleasing to the eye. This interior should acquire not only a new form but even an entirely new artistic quality. We could pass freely through its rooms obeying no other will but our own and enjoying the spectacle displayed before our eyes. The oldest among the churches of the double nave type constructed in Prague have not been preserved in their original appearance being mutilated at subsequent periods. This is especially true of the oldest known double nave church of a longitudinal disposition dedicated to the Holy Ghost. Its double nave was injured by fire in 1499, so that afterwards in the seventeenth century it was shortened by one vaulting compartment. It was founded by a rich Prague burgher Mikuláš Rokycanský about 1346 and should have served as a Benedictine Nunnery.

The second double nave church dedicated to the Virgin Mary na Trávníčku in the New Town of Prague has been preserved in a better state. It was founded in 1360 by King Charles. Its original structure, finished most probably as early as 1378, was so heavily damaged during the Hussite siege of Vyšehrad in 1420 that it became necessary to place a new vault over the double nave which was, however, reconstructed in the same way, thus preserving the original spatial effect. The charm of this church lies in its intimacy which betrays the advent of a new age. The double nave of 2×2 bays is provided with gables, but it is so short that the gables produce rather a picturesque effect, which is still increased by a slender tower placed in front of them. In the interior all the four vaulting compartments are grouped around a central pillar. The interior room seems to be bound to the ground by means of a central pillar, returning thus by its sense, form and quality from the transcendental sphere back into the mundane world, suggesting that man's earthly life apart from his abstract existence is worth living, too; in all this lies the actual purpose of a Czech double nave church.

It was also necessary to adapt the tectonic members of the construction to the newly conceived interior room. Within the choir we still meet with a simple, cylindrical shaft terminating in a cap, for here the necessity of a vertical articulation has survived rather than in the double aisle; the shaft, however, was only carried as far as the window sill. (Similarly as in St. Apollinaris and at the Church of the Virgin Mary na Trávníčku.)

The style was, however, attempting to suppress even the last relics of the tectonic character of the shaft, recalling its formerly supporting function. In the nave of St. James at Kuttenberg we encounter capless and baseless shafts of simple rounded bars running down the pier and ribs passing directly into them. Thus the hitherto-existing logical link between the rib and the shaft was broken in the most sensitive part of the building and the new arrangement of this junction results from the fact that the shaft should belong to the plain mass of the wall and should, therefore, be only perceived optically, having no actual purpose of its own. Such a shaft was employed by Peter Parler in his Bohemianized Cathedral at Kolín (1360—78).

The vaulting corbel was treated in a similar way. The corbel of High Gothic was an actual bracket embedded deeply into the wall and arising from its massive core. As soon as the mass of the wall was changed into an immaterial essence, the massive core disappeared and its form was of no purpose. For this reason the newly created corbels were only applied to the surface of the wall or completely rejected, while each of the ribs was simply undercut. In both cases the corbels are separated from the actual wall by an underlying strip lined with a mid-wall rib which was carried around the entire vaulting support. This way suggests that it is not the core of the wall but its flat surface from which the forms of the ribs and corbels arise. We meet with this arrangement as early as the middle of the XIVth century (Parler's corbel in St. Vitus Vestry, after 1353), but only now they assume forms of a genuinely Czech character which then became a characteristic feature of Czech style even outside Bohemia.

We may, therefore, say that the period of 1360—70 has brought formal maturity to Czech style in two respects. Insofar as the interior room is concerned, its sensual character was attained, whereas both the classical abstract tendency and the post-classical subordination to the altar were rejected. The interior, flooded with light and atmosphere, was related to the world of senses. In contrast to the interior of High Gothic it evoked our feeling of beauty and it became subservient to man, whom it surrounds, when compared to the interior of post-classical type which found its purpose in the transcendental world. As far as the massive body of the building is concerned, its alternation was completed having changed into a weight-less shell formed by walls of purely optic character. The only thing retained from the previous tectonic supply, the ribbed vault, was freed from its dependence upon the rest of the building body and quite freely placed on the shell of exterior walls attached to them only by means of the applied ribs. This new formation of double nave churches arose, expressing a new artistic quality of Czech interior rooms together with new types of vaulting supports so peculiar to the newly created supply of forms. All this was, of course, done rather unconsciously, carried by the feeling or intuition of the artist and yet all this goes to make a logical whole which can only be explained as a direct and spontaneous manifestation of the creative genius arising out of the sensualism of a Czech man.

✳

Towards the close of Charles' reign Czech Gothic style spread over an essentially larger area. The King and royal towns of Central Bohemia were faced with a proud rival, the Lords of Rožmberk who, in the artistic sense as well attempted to surpass them. The original House of Vítkovci fell, in the XIVth century, into four branches; the Lords of Rožmberk, Hradec, Ústí and Landštejn. They took possession of Southern Bohemia establishing their power on economic and colonizing fields, as well as on a number of castles, towns and fortresses which could protect them in military and political situations.

However, it was not only Southern Bohemia that enriched Czech Gothic art at the end of Charles' reign. There was a different district, too, which absorbed many an impulse originating in Bohemia in order to pass it in an altered form back again to Bohemia at a subsequent period: it was Silesia with its capital Wroclaw (Breslau). This country was gained by John of Luxemburg by the treaty of 1327 and when the last Piast Duke, Henry IV died in 1335, Wroclaw actually formed part of the Bohemian Kingdom, which brought about an essential turning-point in the history of this town. It was liberated from its dependence upon Poland and thus also upon the North and joined the Czech cultural sphere of southern type. In the years 1357—69 Wroclaw even became a sort of a town republic paying allegiance directly to the King of Bohemia.

In 1359 Charles built a new castle at Wroclav. At the same time the town-hall was erected, both the parish churches of the town were rebuilt and all the monastic churches were under construction. It is clear that here, as well as in Prague, Charles' reign inaugurated a very busy period of building which was to add to the splendour and outward appearance of the town, besides making good, at least in part, the damage caused by the fire of 1342. In 1377 an attempt was made to introduce building regulations, while founding the New Town, in the same way as was done in Prague. Besides the town itself, of whose wealth and commercial importance the best proof is its membership of the Hanseatic League, there flourished, of course, the whole diocese of Wroclaw, at whose head stood Charles' Silesian chancellor and exponent of Czech politics, Wreczlaw of Pogarell (1341—76). Aeneus Sylvius used no empty phrase when he later called this bishopric a golden one. Owing to the reciprocal ties linking the destinies of Bohemia and Wroclaw, this period of prosperity came to an end at the outset of the Hussite revolution.

While following the development of Czech Gothic up to this point, we witnessed a powerful struggle waged by Czech art in the name of sensually active space against the older stylistic tendencies. We noticed how, under the warm touch of Czech optic feeling, the tectonic features of the classically remodelled wall dissolved into a simpe flat wall and we saw how the wall, too, gradually absorbed all designs with which the post-classic linear style covered its surface. The effort of Czech style was mostly directed to this wall, i. e. to the attack on its tectonic or linear shafts.

What remained outside this struggle was the actual vaulting system. Although the new style denied the wall every tectonic feature, even a mere linear suggestion, on the other hand, it left to the vault its old rib; for Czech Gothic could succeed in mastering the vault in the same way as the wall only at the price of completely abandoning the rib — but such a far-reaching act could not be ventured on by the fourteenth century style. Thus, within the interiors of Bohemian churches, there survives, anchored to the softly rounded bodies of tectonically nude pillars, its detail picked out in broad shafts of light and surrounded by the amorphous face of walls which bear no trace of line or feature, a vaulting system rich in linear features, distinguished by the sharp lines of its ribs, and which lent those interiors a fundamental scheme that preserves tectonic discipline and rhythm that is in keeping with the time-honoured rationalism of the ground-plan. It is natural that it should be this very vaulting chessboard of the ground-plan, so strikingly projected by the vaulting ribs up into space, that was felt by the people of the time to be absolutely unsuitable and an obstruction to their own artistic conceptions; it was as though the age was awaiting the first gallant deed, which should free it from all difficulties in this respect. This historic task was performed by Peter Parler in Bohemia.

The experiment made by Parler in St. Vitus Cathedral in Prague, immediately after his arrival about 1353 expressed his strong protest against the very essence of linear style, against its expressive aim. In violently verticalized clusters of keel-moulded shafts pointing somewhere high up out of the actual building the style endeavoured to express the idea that the content of the building lies not in the building itself but somewhere high up apart from it, in the imagination. It originated, therefore, from the same spiritual atmosphere as the contemporary German mysticism, both relating the meaning of life to unknown imaginary ideas within the infinity of the absolute. It is certain that Parler was already sceptical of such a valuation of life, as his whole work at St. Vitus shows. This effort, which left its mark on all the parts and elements of this great building, was in accord with a similar effort on the part of contemporary Czech style and aimed at denying the vertically rising movement of the building and at breaking it, even to the point of caricature, at the very moment of its culmination. It was, therefore, necessary to create new elements af form: a soft flame tracery for the window and panels which could be bent and curved in any desired direction with perfect smoothness thus making it possible to split the vertical movement of the tracery into several branches or at least to deflect it back and down again, and the pendant which breaks in the same way the movement of the converging ribs, turning it back towards the ground just at the keystone of the vaulting where it culminates. For all this, however, Parler still uses the means available to the linear style, namely richly articulated shafts and mullions.

But he soon realized that it was not enough for his work to consist only of protest and negation, and that positive creation was also necessary, creation towards a new sensual quality in spaces, which was the direction in which the creative effort of Czech style was moving. However, the Rhenish linearism, wherein his art had arisen, did not allow him to start out on the path which was meantime being followed by Czech style and which led finally to the amorphous wall and empty, evacuated space. Parler, on the contrary, continued to reckon with the linearism of shafts and vaulting ribs. He tried at least to soften them and make them gentler to the eye. Since the new Czech style required that the interior space should not derive from the shape of the vault but on the contrary that the vault should accommodate itself to the shape of the pre-conceived space, Parler broke away from the quadrature of the ground-plan of hitherto-existing cross-vaults and aimed at vaults more complete in geometric design which could, by the network of the ribs, better adapt themselves to pre-conceived spatial forms. Thus, for the first time the stage was reached, where spatial form came before the vault and was finally freed from its tectonic hold, just as it had freed itself already in the Czech style from the tectonic hold of the walls. The vault retained its linearism even afterwards, so that it remained distinct in its artistic quality from the empty walls of the vertical spatial cover and lagged behind it in its development, and was stylistically left one step behind.

It is remarkable that Parler again achieved, merely by changing the positions of the vaulting supports in the ground-plan, the formal complexity of the designs which would destroy the tectonic character of the heavy quadratic bays. This artistic feeling could hardly break the inner coherence between rib and support, therefore, the stellar vault is justified in his work only if the special shape of the ground-plan corresponds and naturally gives rise to it. And so, in the Vestry of St. Vitus, Parker did not place the main vaulting shafts at the corners of the interior but in the middle of the lateral walls; in St. Wenceslas Chapel (projected after 1360, finished on the eve of St. Wenceslas in 1366 and consecrated on 30th November, 1367) he placed the vaulting shafs in the two extreme fourths of the walls, and in the adjoining south porch erected at the same time as the St. Wenceslas Chapel and consecrated in 1368, he alternated them diagonally opposite each other. We find a similar diagonal alternation of supports in the choir ambulatory of Parler's Cathedral at Kolín-on-the Elbe (1360—78). Thus there arose complex stellar and half-stellar vaults whose designs are only loosely linked with the predetermined spatial shape, touching it at only a few random points, sometimes even displaced as against the ground-plan proper. So space and vaulting begin now and then to come asunder in their forms.

The principle upon which Parler constructed his complex vaults is not essentially different from that guiding the Swabian Cistercians who built similar vaults before he did. When analysing the Chapter-Hall of the Sázava Monastery we pointed out how these Cistercian vaults differed from the stellar vaults of the northern territories, how it was because of their dependence on the arrangement of the apertures in the external walls and on the diagonal alternation of their supports that the vaults became linked to the shape of the interior as determined by the wall-shell, whereas the actual interior room was freed from dependence on the vaults. The northern vaults, on the other hand, grew out of the interest aroused by their massive detail and its multiplication, i. e. out of the demands of the massive body of the building. This comparison shows what was the true source of Parler's impulse and what was the aim of his vaulting art, which, just as it naturally grew out of Danubian sensualism so it also naturally aimed towards the gates of late Gothic art. Northern art remained alien to Parler because it had nothing to contribute to his artistic searching. There was no essential difference between the vault of the south porch at St. Vitus, which was later, so often and so joyfully, repeated by Czech masters, and the Cistercian stellar vaults at Maulbronn and Bebenhausen. The basic principle of the ground-plan lies in the triangular compartments, which originated in the shifting of the supports and led, when placed next to each other, to the formation of a six-pointed star. The space and vault interlocked, the network of the vaulting became picturesque and its pattern showed more symmetry than the simple cross-vault. Between the front and the back prospect of the porch space, complex spatial relationships arose, carried on the rich play of triple ribbed beams. Thus Parler helped Czech Gothic architecture to free itself from the heavy rationalism of the cross-vault and made the vaulting subservient to the optically over-valued Czech interior.

In Bohemia we witness this diagonally alternate vaulting pattern which soon afterwards produced a picturesque effect by the outlines of their ribs, as we saw in the South Porch of St. Vitus which formed a common model for all of them. This arrangement was especially suitable for porches allowing a structure of two apertures to be placed in front of a single one of the portal so that the longitudinal axis is split. This can best be illustrated by the Porch of the Virgin Mary in the Lesser Town of Prague and by that of the parochial church at Vysoké Mýto, both of them following the example of the St. Vitus Porch. The vaulting pattern of Vysoké Mýto, however, distinct from the one in Prague, is also based upon the diagonally alternate principle. The caps of the local shafts supporting canopied niches bear resemblance to those of the St. Vitus Porch, too. Similarly both of Parler's corbels within the choir (the figures of Adam and Eva and the sculptured representation of the Moon) and the capital of the central pillar of the South Porch as well as the caps of Vysoké Mýto, do not bed into the wall, but are only applied to its surface. Their bodies are attached to the shafts only by a small portion of their profile and strongly project from the wall. The effort of this period cannot be spent on a mere suppression of tectonic character any more but wants to express the revolt against it in a more striking manner, namely in caricature. Similar, excentrically attached corbels may be found on the piers of the Ulm Cathedral in that part which was carried out by the Swabian architect Ulrich of Ensingen (1392—1419), a pupil of Parler's school.

The diagonal alternation of the vaults occur, at that time also, in the Vestry of the Church at Plzeň, dedicated to the Holiest of Holies. It was necessitated by a row of closely spaced buttressing piers projecting from one of its sides. They served as natural supports to the vaults, which, however, finding no corresponding supports on the opposite side were of normal span there. In this way the vaulting supports were shifted diagonally opposite each other and the vaulting design changed into a net pattern, while the capless vaulting ribs bond into that projecting portion of the wall lined with a wall rib.

Besides the net vaults which arose by the diagonal alternation of the vaulting supports, we meet in the Seventies, with a different vaulting pattern resembling a four-pointed star. As it may be found in the buildings carried out directly by Charles IV or in connection with other stylistic elements of the Royal architectural foundation, we suppose that it was modelled on some of Parler's vaults. There is no difference in the ground-plan disposition between stellar and cross-vaults. They differ, however, in the arrangement of ribs, stellar vaults do not form diagonal crosses because diagonal ribs are split here into two. Thus a similar effect was attained here, as with the vault of previous type, the heavy tectonic character of the vaulting compartments stressed by the cross-vaults, was removed.

These types of vaults occur nearly simultaneously in three larger structures of that period: in a passageway of the Lipnice Castle, in the Church at Nymburk and within the choir of the Church at Sadská.

Stellar vaults of the Chapter-Halls provided with central pillars, as exemplified by the Chapter-Hall of the Franciscan Monastery at Plzeň, were likewise constructed upon a diagonal alternation of the vaulting supports. In order to explain their origin we need not trace the influence of the Royal architectural foundation, as they directly follow the example of similar vaults at Maulbronn and Bebenhausen constructed by the Cistercians of Southern Germany. Their artistic purpose was already explained when we examined the Chapter-Hall of Sázava Monastery, wherein this type of a vaulting pattern occurred in Bohemia for the first time. It is, however, of great importance that an arrangement originally resulting from necessity — as was still the case at Sázava — became a form in which artistic purpose prevailed. Stellar vaults of the Chapter-Halls break away from the square compartments of the vaults, forming a fan-like pattern displayed symmetrically around the central pillar which is linked to the corbels placed on the walls by means of ribs radiating from it, resembling fibres of a spider's web.

Insofar as it did not spend its effort in problems concerning vaults the Gothic style of Central Bohemia developed interior spaces upon the principle of a double nave. We have already pointed out that a double nave church best corresponded to the genuine Czech conception of a new interior of sensual quality and that immediately in the beginning this type of church may follow two variations, central and longitudinal. In the period of 1370—80 we witness how quickly both of them found favour throughout Bohemia, being accomplished in form and space. This period was chiefly concerned with the central pillar. It was, no doubt, formally accomplished, too, consisting of a cylindrical body from which spring the capless ribs and yet its proportions were altered; it grew slender, thus suppressing its original tectonic purpose, whereas its space-creating function was emphasized. Unfortunately we know nothing about the proportions of these pillars of the previous period as none have been preserved in their original likeness. In this period (1370—80) the ribs are so extremely slender that they are only about 50 centimetres in diameter whereas their height is 8 meters. Being capless and strongly projecting they resemble hanging, rather than supporting bars. And so finally the Czech aisled hall attained the effect of being supported by only a few small corbels placed on the exterior walls, whereas in the centre it appears to be carried by itself weightlessly touching the ground by means of slender pillars.

A similar effect was produced by the pillars in the double nave of St. Castulus Church in Prague built shortly before 1375, as well as with the adjacent vestry by Pešek of Příboj. Their cylindrical bodies were still provided with octagonal bases whereas the ribs met the upper parts of the pillar by the outmost portions of their profiles.

Pillars of the same type may also be found in the double nave occupying the western part of the cloister belonging to the Franciscan Monastery of St. James in the Old Town of Prague, probably completed simultaneously with the church choir and consecrated by Archbishop John together with the whole monastery on July 6th, 1374. There rounded shafts attached to the exterior walls were surmounted with a portion of string-course. Nowadays, as the double nave is divided by a wall, we can hardly imagine the picturesque effects it exercised, especially if we know that this double aisle opened on the inside into a lovely cloister garth and into a street on the outside. We regret it all the more as it was just the Czech Gothic which successfully adapted the architectural work to human criterion and transformed it into a work of great charm.

For this reason we value so much the parochial Church of Vetlá which has preserved the original likeness of its double nave altogether intact. It sprang up about 1370 as may be judged by the flowing pattern of one of the traceries. The elongated choir opens into the square nave by a widely spanned triumphal arch. The nave of four vaulting compartments is vaulted to a central pillar. The ribs of the cross-vaults are diagonally displaced in front of the triumphal arch. The interior is still strikingly elevated, which adds to the beautiful soaring character of the pillar and triumphal arch — the effort to attain a pleasing, well proportioned form is clearly manifested here, forming an important component of the composition which results from the peculiar aesthetic feeling of the Augustinians at Roudnice who carried out the work.

With the adoption of some of the elements peculiar to Parler's Court style, as were for instance the vaults of diagonally alternate pattern or stellar vaults, Central Bohemia has distinguished itself from the rest of the provinces, especially from the district of Southern Bohemia belonging to the Lords of Rožmberk. Being isolated from the large centres of culture, Southern Bohemia acquired the character of a province as early as the XIIIth century. As the source of its artistic impulses has been rather limited, we can trace here only a small number of fundamental designs developed in simple variations.

Since the very beginnings of the Early Gothic style we miss here that inspiring impulse which may be found only in places where several cultural currents meet. Only such a meeting ground gives rise to new spiritual movements creating them by means of a synthesis of the old ones.

It is, however, very interesting to observe that in Southern Bohemia the period of new building activity in the middle of the XIVth century was not inaugurated by the Lords of Rožmberk, but by the burghers of Hradec. We do not know exactly when they founded the Minorite Monastery at Hradec (the present Jindřichův Hradec). With its construction, however, the architectural history of Southern Bohemia was started. A new, high choir was erected first of all; being of considerable height and elevated, it acquired an extremely dynamic character corresponding to the strictly expressive style of the period.

Some ten years later, in 1369, a new contract, was signed between the monastery and the burghers of Hradec concerning the construction of a cloister. In this contract we find an important allusion to a new chapel, of which the eaves should be repaired; it is St. Nicolas Chapel, still attached to the southern side of the choir, begun about 1365, that is, soon after the completion of the choir. The interior was already determined by its purpose, for it was a bourgeois chapel adjoining a Mendicant Monastery; hence the ground-plan consisted of a square double nave, which by then found general favour in Bohemia, provided with a choir. The diagonal displacement of the cross-vault occurred only in the eastern part of the nave, being necessitated by the windows and especially by the triumphal arch; and so the chapel recalls similar Cistercian designs of which the net pattern may, likewise, be explained from the disposition of exterior walls.

A very simple event gave impetus to a spontaneous outburst of building activity in Southern Bohemia: the Lords of Krumlov, the brothers Jodocus, Peter, Ulrich and John bought the estate of Třeboň from the Lords of Landštejn on September 23rd, 1366, and as early as 1367 they founded a Monastery at Třeboň for the Augustinian friars who came in from Roudnice in Central Bohemia. The construction of the church and cloister was begun immediately after their arrival, for we know that as early as November 1369 the local cloister formed the model for that of the Minorite Monastery at Hradec. It is clear that at least part of the cloister must have been completed at that time.

It was this very monastery that introduced into Southern Bohemia the Gothic style of Central Bohemia in its full development and in the genuine Czech form of a double nave. In tracing the artistic purpose of double nave of this type we have already described how the interior anchored to the central pillars, was centred around them and how its longitudinal character was broken by splitting the axes of the nave and choir. We can observe how the slenderness and fragile elegance of spatial and sculptured forms were increasing. This becomes especially apparent in the soaring proportions of the triumphal arch and in the subtlety of the tall pillars, the height of those at Třeboň being at least 16x their diameter. We have also mentioned that, being so slender, the pillars cannot put their actual function into practice any more, having changed into forms of purely optic effect, so that they appear to be suspended on the vault carrying the sharp lines of the ribs down to the ground. All this is further developed at Třeboň. In order to attain greater uniformity of the interior, the outer compartments of the nave were groined by the vaulting of diagonally alternate principle allowing for an uninterrupted continuation of the vaulting compartments. Thus, also, the two main axes, the one of the nave and the other of the choir, were split in the triumphal arch after a similar manner found in the St. Vitus Porch. It is even possible that the vaulting design was affected by the St. Nicolas Chapel at Hradec where a similar type of vault is to be found, while at Vetlá this problem was solved rather irresolutely in this respect. At Třeboň, however, we witness a new type of vaulting design. The vaulting of diagonally alternating supports was analogously applied in that part of the nave attached to the west gable. This arrangement did not result from the disposition of apertures, as was the case with the triumphal arch, but was of exclusively optic character help-ing to carry the vault continually round the last of the central pillars. The church at Třeboň is of great importance in another respect as well. When tracing the features of late Gothic style in it, we are surprised to find that its interior is altogether of a uniform character having no distinct aisles or other lateral parts. In the period of High Gothic the interior was divided into choir, naves and aisles; each of them being separated by arcades and existing by itself. The height of the shaft within the nave was doubled as against that of the aisles, while the aisle represented a smaller version in relation to the nave; more over each part had artistic purpose of its own, even though all of them constituted the interior of a single church. They were not linked by artistic form but by their spiritual task; that is by their abstract value derived from the field of rational conceptions. The church represented a unity only insofar as its content was concerned. This was also the case with early Gothic painting: the legend was represented in several isolated scenes linked together by their content, that is not by their artistic but narrative function while each scene had its own criterion, perspective and space. The art of the Třeboň masters is of a different character. In the panels of the local altars the first attempts were made to represent the scene as a section of the real world, wherein all objects are joined by the same perspective construction, atmosphere, lighting and criterion, which absorb their abstract quality pertaining to their content and replace it by the sensual. Therefore, the painter depicts the whole of the arranged scene from a single point placed in front of the picture wherefrom it is observed and visually perceived: all the objects are depicted in such forms and with such relative disfigurements as are only justified with regard to that single place of observation. We meet with a similar treatment of space in architecture, only here the case is not to represent, but to create space. In order to observe the whole interior of a church from a single place, that is to appreciate it in its entirety, it became necessary to abandon the type of basilica and to reject the aisles which are enclosed independently and have their own form and criterion.

35

Such an additional composition could only be comprehended when we really pass through the individual parts of the church, gradually perceiving and combining them in our minds. On the contrary, the necessity occurred of creating a harmonious interior in the form of a hall united by the same illumination, criterion and atmosphere; for this reason the double nave of Třeboň is so brightly illuminated in all its parts, filled with so unifying an atmosphere and for this reason also it is of equal height with the choir. Similarly, the panels of the Třeboň master depict lank and unreal figures surrounded with a mysteriously darkened and phosphorescent atmosphere, as if of another world. In church architecture all of these sensually perceived forms are accompanied by the spiritual evaluation of life; in this connection with the world of senses it was probably influenced by the spiritual atmosphere so characteristic of the Augustinian Friars, manifest in the effort to attain vertical character of forms, solemn grandeur and forms of immaterial essence, and striving to ascribe spiritual character to each material part of the building body. If we realize that this renewed spiritual attitude governing the building body is accompanied by delight in a beautiful and pleasing form, so peculiar to the time, we shall be able to explain the refined window traceries within the local cloister, whose patterns are formed by only a few fundamental forms, together with the attractive traceried arches of the vaulting corbels which afterwards became characteristic of the Třeboň style. We can also understand why all the portals built by order of the Lords of Rožmberk in Southern Bohemia imitate the beauty and elegance of those at Třeboň. The building art of Southern Bohemia also borrowed its vertical character, slender pillars and brightness of its interiors from the Třeboň Church, together with its picturesque outlines. It is, therefore, clear that the Třeboň Church stood at the cradle of South Bohemian art, which thus obtained from Central Bohemia its most accomplished style.

The building, provided with a high altar in 1378, was not completed until the Eighties of the XIVth century, since one of its founders, Peter of Rožmberk, endowed it on April 14th, 1380, remembering that it should be groined. It is natural that we meet during this period with forms borrowed from the older stylistic supply of Cistercian type, which was only gradually suppressed by the style of the Třeboň school. The choir of the parochial Church at Bavorov represents such a stylistic relic, lagging behind its time. It was finished in about 1370, flanked by a high slender spire on the northern side. Its ground-plan recalls that of Cistercian type since the actual choir is connected with a transverse wing similar to the Cistercian transept, which was subsequently absorbed by the nave. The choir also betrays its dependence upon the post-classical Cistercian architecture in the stylistic conception of vaulting and shafts, which, both rounded and polygonal, as within the choir at Hradec, are of so immaterial an essence that they resemble mere fibres.

The slender Cistercian forms did not prevail in Southern Bohemia for a long time. Approximately in the seventies, as the individual structures of the Třeboň Monastery followed one another, Southern Bohemia was gradually supplied with a sufficient number of delightful models of Central Bohemian provenience, which found general favour and spread so quickly throughout the land that by the middle of the Seventies we may talk about a special school or group of architects who further developed the style of Třeboň. One of the contemporaneous contracts gives us a deep insight into these affairs, ascribing the leading task in the art of building in Southern Bohemia to the Třeboň works. There is also no doubt about the nationality of the stone carvers, who by then created their masterpieces in the Třeboň style, since their simple biblical names differ from the compound ones of German burghers. On November 9th, 1359, a contract was signed between the guardian John of the Hradec Minorites, brother Vyšemír, and the master-masons Nicolas and Andrew who were employed to erect a cloister and a portion of the wall dividing the church from the dormitory, next to a number of smaller reconstructions. Both of them did not belong to the Třeboň school, as is obvious from the fact that according to the contract they had to follow the Třeboň work which had not been completed and did nor discharge its own people. We notice how the Třeboň forms were introduced into other buildings in direct accord with the wish of the builder, how the local masters adopted them and how the people of Southern Bohemia were impressed by their charm and beauty. As late as the end of the third and beginning of the last quarter of the XIVth century, when the Třeboň double nave had been prepared to be vaulted, its charming interior, together with all of its essential features, especially the enormously slender central pillars, began to be imitated throughout the Rožmberk territory.

The oldest of these imitations belong to the period of 1370—80. In reality it was only the double nave of St. Vitus at Soběslav that was modelled directly on the Třeboň Church at that time. The choir of three bays is attached to the double nave of 3×2 bays. The unusually subtle proportions of its two central pillars (only 40 cm in diameter), the diagonally alternating vaulting corbels, together with the lofty forms are of Třeboň provenience and only the simplified profiles of the triumphal arch and vaulting ribs which abandoned the fully massive forms of keel mouldings and are carved with shallow soft grooves, witness how style proceeded on its way towards the new form of optic effect.

A similar style, tending to picturesque and fragile forms may also be traced within the Chapter-Hall (the so called Draper's Chapel) of the Minorite Monastery at Hradec, constructed about 1375. Its traceried corbels are of Třeboň provenience while the profiles of the ribs recall those of Soběslav. The central pillar, modelled on that of Soběslav, is only 30 cm in diameter, which testifies how subtle a form acquired its body wherein the interior room, groined by a stellar vault, found its centre.

About the year 1374 Peter and John of Rožmberk undertook a reconstruction of the parochial Church at Sedlčany upon a double nave principle (or at least intended to do so). The intention is manifest from the proportions of the nave of which the original vault was demolished and from a portion of the central pillar of 46 centimeters in diameter, preserved in the churchyard of the local church. The Sedlčany Church introduced into Southern Bohemia the square-headed choir, whose purpose is to be found in the protest against the expressive longitudinal tendency of the interior room. This type of choir quickly spread over the neighbouring provinces as may be illustrated by three country churches dating from about 1380: the one at Kondrac of diagonally alternating vaulting corbels, employing the ribs of Sedlčany provenience, the other at Živohoušť of which the triumphal arch is reminiscent of that at Kondrac and the third at Střezimíř.

*

After the death of Charles IV in 1378 no essential change took place in the historical course of Gothic style. Its foundations so carefully built up by Charles IV have already been firmly established, only in its further development we do not meet with Charles' influence as frequently as before; its completion being thus attained without the direct support of his creative personality. In this way we may explain the fact that in the first period of Wenceslas' reign Czech Gothic art developed along similar lines and solved similar stylistic problems as in the previous period. We cannot, however, suppose that the spiritual atmosphere of Wenceslas period entirely resembled the previous one. Owing to two circumstances, the close of the XIVth century became, by its spiritual background, an interesting and rather peculiar period: the first of them is represented by King Wenceslas himself, so essentially distinct from Charles IV, while the second is to be sought in the fact that the spiritual development, inaugurated in the reign of Charles IV, reached its climax towards the close of the XIVth century. The personality of Wenceslas did not obstruct this development; on the contrary, its effort was so fully understood by him that the effects of both of the spiritual forces were doubled. This explains why the Czech spirit had so far completed its development in the last years of the XIVth century that as early as 1400 it could create works unaparalleled throughout the contemporaneous Europe.

From the time of his youth — he succeeded upon the throne at the age of eighteen — Wenceslas appeared to his contemporaries as the very opposite of Charles. Being irritable, hot-tempered and passionate, he never possessed his father's deliberation and firm perseverance; he also lacked the vast knowledge that Charles had in addition to his natural wisdom, his belief in the power of objective thinking and in the absolute order of the world. Wenceslas lived the life of an individual man enjoying his privacy and accessible to emotional excitement rather than to speculation or meditation on spiritual questions. Rationalistic discipline and a sense of the objective, and generally obligatory order were alien to the subjective personality of this incessantly improvising King who was engaged rather in personal experiences, such as the passionate speed of hunting, the buoyant society of several favourites, who were sometimes of low birth, and perhaps even the romance of small adventures, which he enjoyed every now and then. To be brief, Wenceslas belonged to the late Gothic period which, wearied by the hitherto-existing effort, attained its fullest spiritual development and passing beyond it reached the point when the late summer days begin to be pervaded by the first melancholy of autumn.

This period, as it is reflected in creative art, literature, religious and social life, appears to resemble the King himself. The lack of monumentality, together with the decline of Caroline representativeness and symbolic festive pathos are, in Wenceslas' age, counterbalanced by their very opposite — the liking for private life, which could be mastered by man's personality itself. It seems as if life now assumed a bourgeois character even at the Court. We do not meet here with aristocracy of international level but merely with an intimate society claiming some sort of material comfort and enjoying personal delights, passions and other inclinations of man's nature. Human personality was not bound by abstractions or conventions to the same extent as was required by the previous period, especially in the field of art. All this, however, resulted, as a necessary consequence, from the process which caused the spiritual life to depend upon the senses and based the whole of culture upon sensual perception. The humanitarian idea, which came into being, was manifest not only in society from the increasing understanding of social justice, but also in literature from the necessity of psychological motivation of a deed, which should replace the hitherto-existing explanation of historical events from God's will. This idea is also apparent in a new conception of State and social classes which is expressed in the contemporaneous literature by the well-known phrase: the baron is for the community and not the community for the baron, people are born free. In this way the old medieval conception of society built upon the feudal and hereditary relationships was, at least theoretically, replaced by a more modern and democratic idea of equality of all people still, of course, understood from the point of view of Christian learning: that is equality before God. The wave of growing sensualism under King Wenceslas gave rise to an entirely new attitude towards art and to a new function of artistic form. Already in the period of Charles IV we could observe how the artistic form began to be judged by a new criterion, by the sensual feeling of beauty evoked in the perceiving subject. And in the latter part of his reign we met with works of art in which form came before content and in which, therefore, strong aesthetic signs could be traced. The development of art under King Wenceslas followed along much the same lines as in the previous period, only now the aesthetic regard was brought to the point of formal artfulness. Artistic form was suddenly transmuted into a refined form of surprising, attractive tendency, which being further cultivated, acquired so graceful a character that the formerly tectonic, that is to say pre-determined forms, gave way to arbitrary and even unforeseen ones, arising out of improvisation. This playfulness, never lacking the charm of fragility and growing out of the delight in an ingenious and beautiful form, constitutes the most characteristic feature of Late Gothic art about the year 1400, especially insofar as the Prague Court is concerned. We may trace it in architecture, sculpture as well as in painting and book ilustrations, to which a suitable term "greenhouse" art is applied by the art historians on account of their playful character. The quick evolutional progress of Czech art was especially caused by an apparent tension arising at the end of Charles' reign between the popular art, which we have just traced, and between the ornate style of the Court developed by Parler. However Bohemianized, Parler's stylistic form did not abandon its primary elaborate character, that was still reminiscent of its French provenience. On the other hand, the local supply of forms was considerably poorer when compared to the French one, since it followed and kept on reducing forms which had already been simplified. It was not until the time of Wenceslas that both of these styles started to adapt one another. The artistic form of the Court art was simplified, accepting, especially, the plain wall of Czech Gothic architecture, while the domestic style was enriched by many an element adopted from Parler's art, among which belong the new patterns of net-vaults in particular. Apart from this, there a number of buildings in Bohemia, most probably belonging to some masters of Parler's school and yet distinct from it, were constructed. They form an important link between the two above mentioned styles, adding to their mutual coalescence. Among the works suggesting the part of some architect of Parler's school, two belong to the period of 1380—90, both of them being very interesting from the point of style which becomes essentially simplified and visually softened as against that of Parler. It is the Oriel Window of the Caroline University in the Old Town of Prague and the gable of the

Týn Church. The gable, lined with slender finials in place of crockets is covered with a horizontal tier of arcades formed by trefoil traceries; in its centre we find a shallow niche. Below the main string-course of the façade runs a tier of small arches surmounted with fleurs de lys. All the panels, finials and friezes, so peculiar to the late style of Parler's school, are, however, entirely alien to Czech Gothic architecture, as is exemplified by the façade of the Bridge Tower; the manner, however, whereby they are treated, is genuinely Czech. These ornate forms were applied here for the sole purpose of producing the effect of light and shade on the plain mass of the gable. Therefore, as on the contemporaneous façade of the Bridge Tower, so here, the appearance of the building is changed according to the changing sunlight, since ever new optical effects are produced by the cast shades animating the stony and seemingly immobile aspect of the structure. As each of the tectonic forms is accompanied by a number of additional members, such as crockets, friezes, finials covered with natural foliage, which should add to the softening and picturesque character of the rigid geometrical aspect, we sometimes apply the term "soft" to this unreduced late phase of style.

The Bohemianizing process was then further developed in the Nineties of the XIVth century when one of the stonecarvers of the Court built the Oriel Window of the Caroline University. Since the oriel was not roofed, all of the vertical lines, so freely expressed in the Oriel Window of the Prague City Townhall of earlier date (1381), were suppressed here by the crowning stone-work of a balustrade; as against the linear conception of the Townhall façade, the oriel of the University displays broad patches of light and shade on its exterior. The mouldings lining the panels beneath the windows produce a special effect by their dark shades, while the heraldic devices carved in high relief form dark stains on the light face of the background, placed obliquely with the main axis in order not to stress the vertical character of its lines. Therefore, its outline, too, is deeply split: the gargoyles placed at its angles together with the applied canopies jut out freely towards the sky, allowing the greatest possible twilight to be concentrated upon their parts facing the ground. The oriel is supported by corbels applied to its concave softly modelled base. They resemble bars of deeply projecting ribs and being curved several times project deeply from the mass of the oriel. We notice that the art of building is concerned with the problems pertaining to painting, as it operates with similar means as, for instance, modern impressionism. The signs of a complete tectonic relaxation in style may even be traced in Parler's own art as exemplified by the vault within the passageway of the Bridge Tower in the Old Town of Prague. It was erected approximately in the Eighties of the XIVth century; its most interesting feature being the shaping of the lowest parts of the vaults. The individual ribs terminating in sharp apices gradually merge into the plain mass of the inner walls of the tower, being attached to it by the greatest possible portion of their profile. Just for this reason it was necessary to split their course at the bottom of the vault and to cause the individual bars to interpenetrate in order to form a wide, wedge-shaped base into which the central rib bonds. This manner of constructing ribbed vaults in no way corresponded to the tectonic principle and remained misunderstood in Bohemia for a long time. It was not adopted until the middle of the XVth century by the Late Gothic style of Franconia and Swabia in order to model the form of its vaulting supports upon this principle, which also found favour throughout the Danubian district and in Saxony at the beginning of the XVIth century.

A small church, probably erected by some of the Court masters, in the village of Libiše near Prague arose out of the refined atmosphere at the Court, which gave rise to elaborate and almost artfully graceful forms. Inside the church, we trace the beginnings of a style which may be denoted as a bold revolt against the principles of the tectonic order: the rounded or polygonal bodies of the vaulting corbels are applied to the wall face merely by their flanks, hardly touching its surface. Their centres of gravity lie outside the wall. This manner, which is so peculiar to the north portal of the Týn Church should express the concept that the wall, immaterial in its essence, possesses neither coherence nor inner core into which the actual body of the corbel could be embedded. It is, therefore, sufficient to attach the corbel slightly to its surface.

The building art of Southern Bohemia, when compared to that of Central Bohemia, simply developed the forms already adopted in the previous period. Since the Rožmberk domain still formed a separate territory with its own culture and politics, its art of building developed apart from the currents arising out of Central Bohemia; and so its churches could form a homogeneous group, more harmonious from the point of style than before, when the last relics of Cistercian forms still survived. The tradition, which continued to secure a high artistic level to Southern Bohemia, grew out of the Třeboň school. It was not only manifest in the emphasis on verticality lending the local churches a festive character, but also in the preference of the churches for the double nave type, wherein the illuminated interior is anchored to the strikingly graceful central pillars; so far as the forms of choirs are concerned, the older polygonal and the newer squareheaded types alternated here as they already did in the previous period. The parochial church at Miličín, belonging to the Lords of Rožmberk, followed the type of Třeboň at the beginning of the above mentioned decade, as did St. Vitus at Soběslav towards the close of the previous one. The church consisted of a lofty double nave, shortened as against the one at Třeboň, in one twin-bay and also its tower was terminated by a snow-white brickbuilt helmet, as was the case with the majority of the Rožmberk church buildings of the period, this time enriched in four flanking pinnacles modelled on those of the Prague towers.

The parochial church of St. Peter at Soběslav, founded circa 1380 by Ullrich of Rožmberk to whom Soběslav belonged in 1374—90, was also designed on a double aisle plan. The choir, however, extended to 3 bays has, again, a square head, of which the eastern side is pierced with two windows. This new type of choir, already employed at Sedlčany spread all over Southern Bohemia, most probably together with the vaults based on a diagonally alternating arrangement of the vaulting supports within the last of the vaulting compartments; moreover it was essentially elevated which added to the soaring and harmonious character of the interior. The lofty proportions of the Třeboň Church, pervading the entire architecture of Southern Bohemia, prevail here as well. We notice that each of the Rožmberk architectural works usually adopts some of the elements and parts from the previous church buildings, whereby the old supply of forms was enriched. This proves that the builders of the same school operated here with the same supply of forms enriched by their common work and transmuted into a system of types and sculptured forms carved with a few fundamental patterns, since any other way could hardly be followed with such violent building activity. Thus, the firm and remarkably unyielding tradition of Southern Bohemia came into being in the first ten years of Wenceslas' reign. Based on the principal elements and composition of the Třeboň school it was built up, in reality, only by the works of several master architects. It was further developed, afterwards grew strong, and even survived the Hussite wars to reach its second climax in the Late Gothic period.

THE PERIOD OF 1390—1420

With regard to the previous periods this one might appear too long, yet such a division is based on well grounded reasons. In the XVth century the intensity of Czech architectural production was gradually relaxed, the number of new structures decreased and large building operations, then in the process of completion, were stopped. We are simply at a loss how to fix the "terminus ad quem" of this period, for Czech creative imagination had been deeply touched by the anticipation of the Hussite revolution as early as the end of the first ten years of the XVth century.

Thus, in reality the centre of this period must be sought about the year 1400. As often occurs in life, on the very eve of its end, the Czech art of building made such remarkable attemps to strengthen the intensity of its expression that it attained the final aim of the Czech creative genius just at the moment when the first signs of aging appeared in its heart.

All of the attributes which characterized the spiritual maturity of the Wenceslas period refer, in the form of superlatives, to the period about the year 1400; the aim of Czech creative effort was achieved, and the refined Gothic style of Bohemia gained its finishing touches.

Czech Gothic style, developing apart from the Court, found its climax in two groups of buildings closely related to one another, each of them arising out of the artistic experiences of all the previous ones: the first group consists of churches around Kuttenberg, while the second is represented by the architecture of the Rožmberks.

If we eliminate royal building operations at Kuttenberg we shall take here into consideration two almost simultaneously erected chapels, each of them completing the development of Czech style in a peculiar way: the are the Ossuary of the Cistercian Monastery at Sedlec and the Holy Trinity Church near Kuttenberg. The Ossuary is remarkable for its small dimensions and ingenious design. Upon a wide substructure containing the Ossuary, there was erected a chapel of small delicate dimensions resembling rather a precious shrine than a building; the façade is flanked by two towers of slender smoothly carved members. Its square choir together with the sharp pointed windows testify that it is of Cistercian provenience. The ingenuity of its forms, the picturesque character of its appearance and especially its interior of double aisles are, however, peculiar to the Czech Gothic style. In its centre there once stood an incredibly slender and smooth pillar which at the same time formed a keystone of the lower vault. The ribs of the stellar vault sprang from the pillar in a regular manner slowly merging into those portions of exterior walls lined with the wall-rib. As the original vault has not been preserved, we can hardly imagine the perfect beauty of this interior. However, we may at least admire the accomplished form of its ground-plan, its composition entirely based on vertical and diagonal lines, all contributing towards its harmonious whole. The peculiar composition of medieval ground-plans, to which additional bays could be attached without any harm, was completely abandoned. The whole structure is of a uniform character, inside as well as outside, and for this reason also the picturesque towers form but part of its sculptured detail, homogeneous from the point of style. The Sedlec Ossuary constructed about the year 1400 arose from the lucrative activity of the Friars, as each of the rich wanted to be buried inside the crypt, and, therefore, endowed the Monastery with generous legacies.

The Holy Trinity Church completed the development of the Czech aisled hall in another way. It is situated in the former mining district lying to the south of Kuttenberg. Its triple nave was built to a plan which engaged the artistic effort of the Czech style throughout the period of Charles IV; the ground-plan forms a regular square, that is a formation of equal length and width. The entire triple nave is vaulted to four symmetrically placed pillars, while the separating arches of the nave arcades were rejected. However, the perfectly graceful and ingenious forms bear witness to the accomplished style of the aisled hall. The delicate vaults covering the smooth shell of the interior walls are supported by several slender corbels so as not to fall down by their own weight. The four thin pillars resemble suspending bars whereby the entire vaulting system is linked to the ground. In reality the interior represents a large, unaisled hall of four central pillars; the shell of the exterior walls is conceived as a formation distinct from the vaulting and would not be affected by any change, even if they employed but a single central pillar or none at all. This type of interior room is not sub-ordinated to the structual idea of the building body any more and may be modelled as an independent space. Its artistic quality lies in its uniformity; it is filled with the same atmosphere as the actual world of which it forms a part, displaying the sunlit body before our eyes.

A group of subsequent Rožmberk churches developed their interiors at the very borders of the evolutional basis influenced by the local builders of previous years and borrowing, especially the new type of vaulting patterns, from the late style of Parler's works. It would take us long if we were to trace the origin of these network patterns which had long before been in preparation in Parler's style of building and show how their composition and forms were pre-determined by a peculiar function of the structural elements within the walls of the high choir. Suffice it to remember that Parler adopted, in his old age the artistic aim of the Czech Gothic style for his own, attempting to liberate the interior of a church from its sub-ordination to the firm tectonic articulation of the building body, however, under more difficult circumstances arising out of the more complex sculptured forms which he created. The means which helped him accomplish his task were also of a complex character; the vault, suppressed by the Czech Gothic style in that it was of a uniform character with the preconceived interior, became the final aim of Parler's artistic effort; he broke away with its logical composition and tectonic coherence, removing the diagonal as well as transverse ribs. And so, already, within the choir of St. Vitus each of the diagonal ribs was branched into two, whereby the rigid vaulting patterns were considerably softened and the coherence of the transverse ribs spoilt. Moreover, in the line of the longitudinal axis in place of key-stones there appears a continuous band of small rhombic vaulting cells running throughout the vaulting compartments regardless of their division, with the result that the separate vaulting patterns softly mingle together. Parler's vaults of network patterns still calculate on the effect of the geometrically conceived ribs, lending, however, an unusual beauty to its outlines of freely flowing rhythm, as was required by the "soft" style of the last years of XIVth century.

The St. Vitus choir was completed in 1386 and five years afterwards we meet with a similar vaulting pattern in the Vestry of the parochial Church at Milevsko in Southern Bohemia. Its fabric was built to a usual plan of double nave of the Třeboň type from which it also adopted the vertical character of its proportions together with its refined forms. Being white and smooth, the church produces a picturesque effect, erecting its body with a Romanesque tower high above the surrounding walls. Its sunlit interior is brilliant and was once covered with a similar vault as is still found at Třebon. The vault within the choir is, however, of a new type occurring here for the first time in this period. It is based on a similar principle as that of St. Vitus, only here the vaulting pattern is formed by a six-pointed star passing from one vaulting compartment into another without conforming to their arrangement. With the church of Milevsko, two types of network pattern are being introduced into Southern Bohemia, giving rise to a new method of vaulting which remained in operation throughout the subsequent fifty years, especially in the adjoining Danubian district.

On the other hand, the parochial Church of Klatovy is pervaded by the tradition of Bavorov, whose choir was built to a cruciform plan. It was started towards the very close of the XIVth century, as we can judge from the Papal Bulls of 1399 and 1400, and completed in 1414. The stylistic tradition of Southern Bohemia is manifest here in the network pattern of its vaulting as well as in the liking for that type of double aisles. The choir is placed cross-wise with the line of the longitudinal axis after the manner of a transept the origin of which is to be sought in the former Cistercian tradition of Southern Bohemia. The bars of the shafts running down the walls are lined with wall ribs; in some places, however, we meet with a shaft which is curved immediately below its cap and bonds into the wall. As some of the wall ribs are terminated in a similar way we may judge that there is a connection between this church and that of St. Stephen in Vienna, where similar forms accur as well.

In tracing further evolutional relationships we are led from Milevsko directly to Krumlov the capital of the Rožmberk domain. Documents found in archives also testify that the Church of Milevsko played the leading role in the development of South Bohemian art of building. Ulrich, the last of the four above mentioned brothers, united the entire Krumlov territory under his reign and when he died in 1390, his son Henry, who was afterwards appointed Lord Chamberlain and Burgrave of the Prague Castle, moved to Krumlov (he died in 1412). During the last years of his reign he carried out a number of reconstructions: the Palace of the Krumlov Castle including a new private chapel was rebuilt and a new parochial church, dedicated to St. Vitus, was begun. The actual initiator of this new church was Hostislav, the parson of Krumlov, who represents the most outstanding personality in the political life of Krumlov especially after Henry's death. The contract of the 22nd April 1407, concerning the construction of the vaults was concluded between Hostislav and a certain builder, John. We learn from it about the organization of the Rožmberk workshop, about the individual masters who usually belonged to the same family of builders. Moreover, the Czech names of the builders bear witness to the fact that already at that time there existed Czech families of builders who, passing the art of building from generation to generation, preserved the remarkably reserved tradition of Southern Bohemia, of which the highest achievement is represented by the Krumlov Church. In the artistic conception of the Krumlov Church several traditions and spiritual currents combined, which contributed to the surprising beauty of its forms. It was the old tradition of the Augustinian Friars above everything else, introduced into Southern Bohemia with the Třeboň Church and lending something from its sensually intoxicating atmosphere and optic charm to each of the Rožmberk building operations. The interior of the Krumlov Church seems to be picked out by light and shade; its sculptured forms are soft, and smooth, the plain wall made brilliant by shafts of light streaming through the wide windows produces a similar effect as the vaulting. Moreover, the solemn verticality of both the interior and exterior which is so peculiar to the exalted spiritualism of the Augustinian spirit and of the whole of the XIVth century, only adds to the soaring and immaterial character of every sculptured form. We may trace it within the choir, in the triumphal arch as well as in the slender bodies of the piers, while on the exterior it pervades the buttresses, the steep roof provided with picturesque rafters and a slender octagonal tower placed in front of the nave gable. A rich play of light and shade is displayed on its façade by sun remodelling the sculptured forms of buttressing piers by means of narrow shafts of dazzling light caught upons its flanks, which adds to the pictorial effect of white walls and coloured roof. All this may already be found at Milevsko, as it arose out of the optic style of the Třeboň Church; within the Krumlov Church this style was brought to the point of a refined accomplishment. The artistic quality of its interior, arranged so as to be grasped at a glance, is also of the Třeboň provenience. For this reason the jambs of the triumphal arch were removed and the piers within the nave, still supporting narrow arches, are of an extremely slender character. On the other hand, however, the interior retained its subordination to the altar so peculiar to the XIVth century, expressed by the prevalent longitudinal disposition of the church. The walls are plain and smooth, only within the choir which has no pillars, there are slender shafts of bell capitals attached to the wall in order to stress its vertical lines. The vaults, however, belong to quite a different system of forms. Their network patterns, rich in geometrical outlines differ from the empty walls in an effective manner. They were borrowed from Parler's style, together with the flame-traceries: as within St. Vitus, here too the rigid arrangement of vaulting squares was removed and the individual vaulting patterns mingling together and, interpenetrating, formed a continuous band, accommodated to the predetermined length of the interior room. Each rib af the cross vault is replaced here by two running parallel which adds to the optic softening of its tectonic forms. And so, by borrowing the network pattern from the style of Parler, the Krumlov Church obtained the most developed stylistic form it could attain at that time. Moreover we must take into consideration the refined playfulness of the late Gothic period. Formalism is brought to art, artistic production began to change into a play with form. The logically conceived forms of optic effect gave way to ingenious playthings wanting to surprise or only amuse the spectator by their unexpected forms. We may observe these forms inside the church, in the youngest part of the nave, e. g. in the springing of the triumphal and arcade arches which rest upon a string-course placed across the angle; the fundamental tectonic forms started to interpenetrate.

A similar feature may be traced in the bases of the piers, where the individual mouldings of a string-course interpenetrate as well; even the piers themselves became the object of a momentary caprice or fancy, their octagonal bodies alternate with those consisting of four semicylinders. As soon as the architectural form had abandoned its tectonic style and was transmuted into a merely decorative form, it found itself in the sphere of improvisation and could not be prevented from assuming the most phantastic appearance in order to attract attention and curiosity. It is, therefore, decorativeness, that distinguished the Krumlov Church from the artistic effort of the XIVth century, inaugurating thus the period of Late Gothic style. It represents the synthesis of the hitherto-existing stylistic forms, suggesting at the same time their future development.

Its is very interesing to observe how even the abstract spirit, so peculiar to the Cistercians, became subjected to this general playfulness of the time. The parochial church included within the building operations carried out by the Zlatá Koruna Monastery is of similar significance as the Ossuary at Sedlec. It was built in the local village about 1400 or afterwards and was dedicated to St. Margaret. Its small fabric consists of a double nave provided with two octagonal pillars and a square choir. Cistercian custom is mingled here together with the traditional building art of Southern Bohemia, as is exemplified by a slender octagonal tower, surmounting the eastern gable of the nave. All these are but common facts explicable from the hitherto-existing development; surprising, however, are the triangular concave voids formed at the angles of the nave. We would hardly be able to explain them if we did not know that it were just the Czech Cistercians who so frequently transformed the buttresses into sharp-pointed triangular formations; they are in keeping with the peculiar Cistercian striving after the immaterialisation of tectonic forms, transmuting them into formations of sharp outlines. Here, however, in the Chapel of St. Margaret the buttresses acquired such large dimensions that they penetrated the building body and became apparent in the interior where they formed part of the vaulting design. Thus arose a formalistic and decorative formation almost ungothic in its conception, resulting from a momentary whim. We notice that quite a new formalistic attitude towards the building body came into being at Krumlov which is obvious from the manner in which the ground-plan is linked to the stellar patterns of the vaults, arising out of them and adopted to them in its proportions. The development of this new relation of the vaulting to the building body may be followed afterwards in the XVth century throughout the Salzburg-Bawarian area.

Finally, we shall describe the monastic Church at Panenský Týnec near Louny belonging within the sphere of Parler's style. It was built after a great fire, which in 1382 destroyed the former building; however, as early as 1410 the building progress was stopped on account of a general uncertainty of the time and it was never completed. The church represents a compromise between the Czech Gothic art of building, on the one hand, and the older tradition of the Franciscan Friars on the other. It is a simple aisled hall built to a square plan attached to an oblong choir, of which the walls are covered with shafts of geometrical character. The south portal was conceived as an independent formation, which is a typical feature of Parler's style. Its distinct features appear when we compare it with the south portal of St. Vitus Cathedral or with that of the Týn Church, both forming its model. The rounded columms of St. Vitus or the polygonal shafts of the Týn Church were rejected; their bodies appeared to be too massive and their caps too classical. On the contrary, the smooth jambs of the portal at Panenský Týnec are covered with high shallow niches containing canopies supported by slender shafts. The slender, yet complex forms of the canopies and caps are in sharp contrast to the plain wall, upon which the rich play of light and shade is again displayed. Moreover, even the minutest form is of such a refined and accomplished character that we must unvoluntarily think of the unknown carver and of his liking for these filigree things which he carved. This increased playfulness marks the end of the optic form of Parler's school.

The masterpieces of the last Czech school occurred at the very end of this period, when artistic effort in Czech Gothic style attained the highest degree of formal perfection in the south as well as in the centre of the country, at a time when its artistic purpose seemed already fulfilled. This school not only combined the best of its twin branches, the one native Czech, the other courtly Bohemianized, but it brought their form and content to the point of caricature, by so doing swiftly ending any further evolutional possibilities remaining therein. This school, serving Wenceslas' private ends, betraying its adherence to a Czech programme and, therefore, its indisputably Czech origin in the simplicity of all its forms, followed a road in which all the hitherto-existing effort of Czech Gothic combined to form such a subjective and, at the same time, so extremely sensual a style that in remainel unequalled in European art for a very long time afterwards. Not until a century later did some south German masters achieve nearly the same degree of tectonic relaxation in form as had already been attained in Bohemia about 1400. It is undoubtedly true that the Czech masters followed the example of the St. Vitus school, left them by Parler's successors, displaying their master's sculptured elements in an equally improvising manner. However, their art was supplied with an energy derived from a source foreign to Parler. It arose from a purely Czech source in which Czech creative imagination flourished successfully.

Their first efforts at the Castle of Krakovec already show that it is necessary to seek the beginnings of their art in the period when their inheritance, derived from the older masters as a legacy of King Charles' time, was already at its maturity. This castle was built by order of John, son of the Rhenish Count Palatine Ralph, with the financial support of his brother-in-law, Emperor Charles, some time after 1363, when he bought the local fort and estate. The building, consecrated in 1384, was not completed until the time of Wenceslas' reign. If we pass through its vaulted rooms, only one of which retains its original vault in entirety, we are soon surprised by the irregularities of these vaults. We notice it in some other cellars also, and it is most striking if we can ascend to the first floor of the castle to the former chapel. This part of the building is erected on an oblique unrectangular plan, and the floor of the chapel is, therefore, rhomboid in shape, with alternate obtuse and acute angled corners, caused by the general arrangement of the building. But what of its vaulting? According to the dislocation of small corbels upon which the vaulting ribs once rested, we should expect to find the floor of this vault also to be rhombic in shape, but in fact we have two completely regular rectangles. These were attained so that at both obtuse angled corners of the room, the vaulting corbels were set farther from the proper corners of the room, so that between the areas of vaulting and the slanting walls there arose two artistically empty triangles. It is obvious that here also the vaulting is considered to be only a subordinate insertion set freely on the predetermined shell of the four walls of the building, i. e. quite in the spirit of artistic principles of Charles' time The ground-plan, i. e. the proper formal basis of both these formations, the spatial shell and the inserted vaulting, was always one and the same in the time of Emperor Charles. At Krakovec we suddenly notice how this unity is spoilt: the space surrounded by sloping walls is different from the vault that has been designed on a rectangular plan: the vaulting system in position to the exterior walls all at once does not correspond with it in form. The close relationship between space and vault, upon which the whole development of Gothic architecture had until then stood, was ended and space begins its independence in life.

What is the proper role of space now when in these circumstances it must have lost its original significance? The vaulting itself answers this question, if we notice the positive results brought about by this unusual solution.

It is clear that its role was due to the absolute regularity and symmetry of its forms based upon the geometrical exactness of its curves. The positive result of this solution, with regard to the vaulting itself, is thus the optic and simultaneously purely formal aesthetic value anchored in aesthetic sensual satisfaction; purely sensual beauty was the aim here as a result of the absolute regularity of the spatial design of the vaulting ribs.

The aesthetic demand, which is thereby raised to a leading role in art and which, in our case, brought about the end of the tectonic system of the vaulting ribs being based without harm on the preconceived irregular ground-plan, is suddenly shown to us in this light as artistically stronger than the natural tectonic coherence whereby the vaulting had previously been linked to the building, and it even represented to us as the leading and primary architectural principle on which the artistic sense of the building is established.

In this sense the vaulting itself was, in fact, a mere addition serving only an aesthetic purpose, placed in the preconceived space of the chapel, as we can see by the shape of its choir. It is formed by a polygonically terminated shell, resting on a corbel table supported by a robust buttress rising up along the entire height of the castle façade. There would be no obstruction if at least the choir with its buttressing support joined the façade at right angles, in the direction of the chapel vaults, as we should naturally expect. In reality, however, it is quite different: because the proper chapel space, i. e. that part surrounded by the walls and which played an important part in the eyes of the people of those times, was derived from a rhombic plan, so that even the oriel window stood obliquely in relation to the façade, and the entire left portion logically, but at first sight incomprehensibly, merged into the bulk of the outside walls of the castle. We notice that it is not the vaulting but the exterior walls of the chapel that determined the shape and character of the interior, to which the choir also was obliged to adapt itself. In the time of Emperor Charles such a solution was hardly possible at all.

If we seek the origin of this spatial conception we cannot but remember those remarkable experiments carried out by the St. Vitus school at the local vestry and St. Wenceslas Chapel. There also, as we already know, the interior space is separated from its vaulting and vice versa that the vaulting is a simple interpolation, already considerably independent of the ground-plan of these rooms. If we compare it to the chapel at Krakovec, their mutual relationship is, here, still closer. The ground-plan of the chapel at Krakovec shows no signs that the vaulting should be taken into consideration at all: its ribs are placed everywhere on corbels, so that they do not reach to the ground, while within St. Vitus the interior is still enclosed by the hoops of the ribs which rise unbroken from the ground up to the vaulting in sharply drawn fashion. This absolute loosening of all relation and coherence with the shell of the space was first attained in the vaulting of the Chapel of Krakovec.

Some stylistic elements, found at Krakovec, can also be derived from St. Vitus Cathedral. This is true, above all, with respect to the shape of the local vaulting corbels. They are simple conical segments, bare and slightly concave with sharp pointed apices: their upper parts are only rough-polished and so lack any profile. The cluster of wedge shaped ribs joins the corbel only by a narrow portion of their points: they follow the example of those of St. Vitus, in the so called Upper Passage above the triforium, where they carry the window profiles of the high gallery, covered by allegorical sculptured details. Their origin is definitely between 1373—75, and so we now know the earliest temporal limit to the building of the Krakovec Chapel, which was not completed until 1384.

Within the cellar rooms of the castle we shall however find another equally marvellous method of vaulting. The consequences of the irregular ground-plan of these halls whereby the geometerically exact course of the vaulting ribs would be spoilt, are here equalized at the very bottom of the vaults. This happens naturally on account of their tectonic shape: the vaulting rib rising above the longer of the diagonals in the ground-plan compartment joins the wall much higher than the rest of the ribs, so that it misses its corbel. If we realise how easily all the previous periods levelled these formal irregularities in the vaulting itself where it was not possible to notice them and how, on the other hand, they now cause such violent conflicts at the bottom of the vaults that the irregularity and casualness of these forms at once strikes us, we cannot suppress the feeling that this formal overvaluation of the consequences resulting from the irregularity of the ground-plan is consciously and intentionally sought for, and that immense artistic emphasis is here exerted upon them. A regular, visually beautiful course of the vaulting curve is attained here even at the cost of completely destroying the tectonic coherence of the ribbed cluster at the bottom of the vault, as well as its natural connection with the vaulting corbel: instead, the vaulting supports are completely casual, as if they were the result of a mere momentary caprice. The tectonic discipline which governed all the hitherto-existing developments of the vaulting and the firmly established order were abandoned and gave way to improvisation and unstable, capricious and arbitrary compositive power.

Some of these innovations are also found at the Castle of Točník. The main palace already has a rectangular ground-plan whose design does not allow the existence here of such eccentric conflicts as occurred at Krakovec. If, however, we look at the principal hall situated on the first floor of the building, we find that aesthetic effect was, above all things, taken into consideration here, based on precisely semicircular, mellowed and widely spanned vaults, which have essentially no rising tendency. The aestheticism of the time in conception of the vaulting and its mission is especially striking here. The vaulting corbels should suggest that here, also, the vaulting by its entire massive system is separated from the shell of the exterior walls which create the proper space. The corbels are again conical as at Krakovec, without profile in their upper parts, one of them being covered by rich sculptured detail of slender crockets resembling the contemporary drolleries of book illustrations; their upper edges are not, however, semicircular but three-quarter-circular in shape. These corbels only join the surface of the wall, having their centre of gravity outside the wall mass. This eccentric placing of the corbels can again be noticed in the older works of the St. Vitus school, especially at the north door of Týn Church.

In the sidelhalls of the Palace at Točník, we come across quite another type of corbel. They also are eccentrically attached to the wall surface, as in the main hall, and they likewise have no string-course termination; their design resembles pyramids which under each separate vaulting rib form polygonal fans which merge deeply into the mass of the corbel.

The material coherence of their mass was spoilt, of course, by such an arrangement; the corbels go to meet the valuting ribs by projections of their bodies and so are adapted to them in their articulation and direction, therefore they lose their logical symmetry and formal independence. The formal relaxation of the architectonic member brought to the point of casualness and chance is here again complete.

The reconstruction carried out by King Wenceslas IV at the Prague Castle followed stylistically the example of the vaulting of Točník Palace: we remember, above all else, that part of the ground-floor building of the northwest transverse wing of the King's Palace built by Charles IV, known as the "Pillar Hall". Its style is also to be seen in a smaller hall which is to be found in the main part of the palace, as well as in the narrow transverse wing which Wenceslas had had erected at the east end facing south, i. e. the townward façade of the palace.

The improvising style of the Točník school culminates in the Pillar Hall of Prague Castle. The last relics of tectonic discipline are sacrificed to the optically beautiful curves of the diagonal ribs, the profiles of which penetrate one another at their intersections, according to late Gothic usage, which is particularly obvious in the corbels at the source of the vaulting. Some of them are split into several lobes which break up the massive coherence of their compact mass by deep notches which form irregular wedges; they project from the wall irregularly, meeting the ribs which bond into the walls at unequal intervals. In this way the corbel attains such striking irregularity that its shape has something that, in itself, is almost suggestively phantastic and which continually strikes the spectator by its illogicality, thus demanding his concentrated attention. There also are, however, the corbels whose shape cannot be explained by rational reflection at all, and which, therefore, lack logical explanation — so removed are we now from the rationalism of High Gothic, for instance, the finely designed corbel whose elongated unsymmetrical pyramid carries three ribs, the outer of which can, however, in no way fit into shape — their profiles flattened horizontally, point freely into space, attached to the upper surface of the corbel by only a fraction of their profile. The instability of these constructions, ostentatiously exhibited to the astonished spectator, already definitely calculates on the deception of his senses: the architects here operate with purely illusive means, raising to the level of permanent artistic expression what is otherwise momentous but improvised, temporary and provisional composition. Thus improvisation became a means of attaining a permanent architectonic form whilst eliminating all that till then had been comprehensible and monumental.

If we take this standpoint we shall also understand why these peculiar origins of vaulting, whereby the hall vault is bonded to both the central pillars, could be attained here. Some ribs bond into the mass of the pillar at odd heights and directly as if these pillars were misplaced, giving no room for an ordered end to the vaulting ribbing. Others, however, do not bond into their surface at all but are extended as though it were necessary to link these pillars closer together. If we did not know that these very pillars were the starting-point in the actual-building of these vaults, and that the highest irregular rings from which the ribs branch in such a peculiar way, were carved beforehand, we should be inclined to believe that the architect and mason began these vaults high up, starting near their crowns and proceeding downwards in regular curved ribs to the point where the ribs meet their respective pillars, when the complete error of their conception became obvious to all. Such is the illusive and suggestive effect exerted on the logical and rational spectator by this peculiar and incomprehensible system. All that encloses space here in such an improvissing and casual manner contrasts with customary attributes of festive monumentalism: there is nothing symmetrical, logically perfect or regular which could be based on objective order and collective security. It is interior space that was intentionally deprived of calm, deliberate perfection, intimate and wholly accommodated to human criteria and character by dimensions, massiveness and care-free casualness, as well.

This consciously inaccurate style which shows in each of its parts, as well as its total composition, that it is no more concerned with comprehensibility and order, that it consistently despises a logical and reasoned shape, laughing at the rules of architectural composition and upsetting the logical vaulting system — this revolting and capricious style which knows no bounds, culminates in the chapel which is supposed to be the most precious heritage from the days of Wenceslas, it is the Chapel of the Italian Court at Kutná Hora. In the nave we can find vaulting bases and ribs approaching in profile and design those of the north portal vaulting of the Týn Church and of the Pillar Hall of Prague Castle. The destructive character of this style is further strengthened here, for in place of simple corbels there are rounded shafts with bell capitals, i. e. pseudo-tectonic form. Rib intersects rib in marked contrast to the character, as we have seen at Krakovec, so that both ribs here meet away from the capital of the shaft. In other places, however, the rib causes an extra lobe to be added to the capital to meet it when, by reason of its curve, it does not rest on its proper shaft but remains detached and keyed to the wall elsewhere. The central pillar carrying the nave vault likewise resembles those of the Pillar Hall of Prague Castle: all the ribs bond directly without a small corbel of its own. We cannot avoid the impression that such a solution is rather wilful, obstinate and capricious by its impossibility of explanation, and cannot be accepted as general in such an age of concentrated subjectivism.

But these stylistic peculiarities are far from being the most substantial that bring European magnificence to the Royal Chapel of the Italian Court at Kutná Hora, There is still something more important which raises the entire chapel to the level of first class creative work. Let us look at the ground-plan of its nave: on the one hand, there is an oblong spatial cover elongated in a striking manner and considerably irregular in its ground-plan form, but on the other hand the vaulting is so perfectly regular being based on such richly treated stellar patterns that another, but precisely square ground-plan, can hardly be imagined here. Thus, a dramatic but artistically effective conflict is here arrived at between the irregular interior space and the regular vaulting, the result of which is a mere illusion: it was necessary to cut out a complete side of the regular pattern of the vaulting star so that it might fit the rectangular ground-plan, with the result that the vaulting pattern appears to extend in imagination beyond the exterior walls, i. e. beyond the massive cover. Thus for the first time in medieval architecture there occurred the concept that the vaulting insertion be treated as a section of a larger pattern, extending beyond the real limits of the given space. It is obvious that whatever the cost, the architect wished to attain that impression of perfect beauty whereby the effect of the complex stellar vaults was exercised on the people. The vault of the Sedlec Ossuary was the most important one among them. Having supplemented the original design with extra ribs, the architect transformed it into a rich formation which in its absolute aesthetic validity can also be applied where the area and shape of the given space are inconvenient. It is, therefore, apparent that it was no longer the interior of the chapel, but the aesthetically unusual and effective vaulting formation which became the starting-point of the entire ingenious composition: only a beautiful design, evoking a deep impression on the spectator, and aesthetic effect caused by illusion, i. e. by extremely subjective means, were emphasized.

The oriel window of the chapel has a small net vault in its interior whose model is known from the artistic legacy of the St. Vitus school. Externally, it is a unique type of this sort. An elaborate quadrangular string-course supported by two corbels rests on a robust pier. The foliage of these corbels repeats, so exactly, the foliage of the corbels at Točník that we cannot doubt that the authorship in both these buildings is identical. The quadrangle then carries the polygon of the oriel; its partly projecting shell can be seen only in the upper parts of the building, whilst its lower part is covered by two blind wings formed by a somewhat transparent coulisse which transforms the building into a quadrilateral shape. This solution is unusually interesting as regards our knowledge of the period. For the first time in our architectural history the exterior of the building is divorced from its interior and so the principle on which the existing development was based is, therefore, broken. Quadrangular in its essence, and optically fitting to the rest of the façade, the exterior does not correspond here to the polygonal shape of the interior of the building. Their harmony is spoilt, as well as their logical coherence: empty voids arose between them, spatial hollows filled with the blind coulisse of purely formal interpolation. The theatricality of such an arrangement is obvious at first sight, but at the same time it is also a purely baroque solution which we meet in our country a second time, but not until the period of the developed style of the XVIIIth century.

It is natural that these architectural works whose artistic content we have already examined, should by reason of their non-tectonic qualities and formal relaxation, have a revolutionary effect on their own era. A few dates on which we can base their beginnings prove how quickly they followed one another in swift succession. The Krakovec Castle is the oldest, being completed about the year 1384 when the chapel was consecrated. The Točník Castle was founded in 1394, i. e. soon after the King's release from imprisonment by the nobility and in 1404 it was already inhabited; it, therefore, also belongs to the very end of the XIVth century. The Wenceslas restoration of the Prague Castle is not easy to date. We only know that it took place soon after 1383 when the King moved away to the new court, at what is now the Powder Tower. On the other hand, we know that the Chapel of Kutná Hora was ready in 1400, for the King gave orders for masses to be said there daily, whether he was present or not. With these dates we cover the stylistic development whose outlines we have been analysing, and can date it definitely as of the last twenty years of the XIVth century.

There is, however, another Wenceslas' castle which should belong to the family of buildings mentioned here, adding to our incomplete knowledge of the workshop and its craftsmen. It is Wenceslas' New Castle near Kunratice, erected by the master Kříž in the years 1411—1412. The building process is admirably and precisely described in documents found in archives. The foundations were, however, excavated only from a few of the buildings which by their rectangular plan fit well into the family of castles described here, although their plans and elevations remain unknown to us. According to a few fragmentary discoveries (the jambs of a fireplace) it is probable that this artistic effort whose development we have just followed stylistically culminated here in this, the youngest of Wenceslas' castles. We can also suppose, certainly without well grounded reason, that is was the Czech master Kříž, himself, to whom the King entrusted the erection of this castle which he liked above all others, and that Kříž was, after all, related to that artistic personality which pervaded the older Wenceslas' castles, even though there was more than a decade between the construction of this new castle and that of Točník or the Italian Court.

In the meantime Queen Sophia, the second wife of Wenceslas, since the year 1389, also employed the masters of Wenceslas' architectural foundation in her eastern dower estates. We, therefore, find their work at Chrudim as well as at Dvůr Králové. At Chrudim a large reconstruction of the royal castle was begun about 1402. It was situated in front of the old part of the town over the upper gateway, towards the moat. It is difficult to imagine its appearance in reality, as only a few buttress piers have been preserved. It is, therefore, probable that the royal architectural foundation of Prague took part in the completion of the parish Church of Chrudim, built close to the castle walls. In the time of Queen Sophia only the nave walls and the vaults of the triple nave were being built, but to a considerably changed plan: the style planned for the arcade columns was abandoned, and in order to secure a more unified but spacious church, the height of the aisles was doubled, so that the older corbels which dated from King Charles' time, set meanwhile, now were in a position along the centre of the wall. This part of the building bears typical traces of the Prague masters; there are unsual corbels in the nave attached like mushrooms to the surface of the wall and provided with suggestions of flattened tracery without the crowning tablets. At the angles of the nave they are wedge-shaped, connected by a narrow portion of the string-course. In the nave there are remarkable little coronets set in small pointed arches and surmounted by battlements of fleurs de lys, the whole forming the capitals of the columns in the nave. A similarly designed frieze is to be seen on the older arcade shafts by the west wall of the triple nave. Both the older northern and the later southern church porches bear witness to the craft of the Royal architectural foundation, for in their arrangement as well as in their separate constituent parts, they exemplify the same treatment of forms characterized by the style of the Pillar Hall in Prague Castle. For the first time, however, the basic plan of the building is interfered with in disturbing fashion, with the obvious, but striking intention of merging directly into its masonic core. The front wall of the porch, possessed like Parler's porch of a central pillar opposite the normal door opening, was, therefore, extended outwards to form a triangular, spatially planned formation. Both of the arcades were thus realigned along their axes and made to converge towards a spectator, with the result that their walls gained by softer illumination and better perspective. The alternation of the ground-plan of the porch led, of course, to a new arrangement of the diagonally alternate star pattern vaulting, which, as in the vaulting of the St. Vitus South Porch, employs quadrant shaped ribs which, as we can see in the centre and corners of the wall bond into the wall irregularly. In the tectonic relaxation of its members, this porch shows a striking relationship to the Pillar Hall of Prague Castle, and we may, therefore, date it as being circa 1400.

Richly decorated coronets, which at Chrudim occupy the position of capital ornament upon the columns of the nave, occur again in another church built at Dvůr Králové by the same architectural foundation. This was also established by Queen Sophia. The older Romanesque building erected by the castle walls was demolished about 1400 and replaced by a new building. As it was unnecessary to pay much heed to the older building, except for some portions of the outside walls, the Prague masters could display their talents far more freely than was possible at Chrudim: we are already familiar with their spatious programme from the Pillar Hall of Prague Castle, so that we are not surprised to find here a developed aisled hall with a unified, but artistically effective interior pierced by four slender, but symmetrically arranged central pillars. The friezes forming their capital ornament remind us of the coronets in the Chrudim Church. Smooth walls to which the vaulting ribs are so delicately but simply keyed, the whole interior being filled with light by which one may appreciate it in its entirety, the subtle fragility of its refined form and the view of the vaulting ribs displayed in all their grandeur — these are typical signs of a Czech hall church, confirmed by yet another, that of the Holy Trinity at Kutná Hora. In this period the Czech style fulfilled its historical task, especially when within the choir the shape of the vaulting was distinct from that of the ground-plan of the walls.

At Jaroměř, the dower estate of Queen Sophia which she began to occupy in 1399, the local Augustinian order was building a new monastic church with a spacious aisled nave, short in length but lofty, as were most Augustinian churches. Founded in 1404, but not completed until a very much later date, owing to the outbreak of the Hussite wars, this church was not entrusted to the masters of the King's Royal architectural foundation, since old local traditions related to Silesia and comparative artistic self-sufficiency did not allow the employment of foreign masters. So it came about that in place of the Czech hall the aisled hall of Wroclaw was employed here at Jaroměř — close ties bound the Augustine friars of Jaroměř to Wroclaw, particurlaly to the local Augustinian Monastery of St. Mary Na Písku. It was this very church, with its diagonally alternate arrangement of the vaulting, sparing use of arcade supports, the heavy lines of the buttresses which follow close upon each other, and with the form of its choirs developed at a single level of depth, that served as model for the church at Jaroměř. It was considerably reduced in scale and thus Bohemianized and transmuted also in its east part, where like the Týn Church in Prague, there is a buttress at the axis of each of the choirs in place of a window. Thus, at the very end of the "Czech" century and almost on the eve of the Hussite wars there appears on Bohemian soil a building wherein the artistic milieu of Silesian Wroclaw returned what 40 years ago had been borrowed from Prague architecture; the diagonally alternate net vault transformed into the means whereby we are enabled to realize that long sought ideal of our art: the unified and optically active space filled with light.

✳

If we were asked for the briefest characteristic or the most essential feature of Czech art in the period around 1400, we would stress that Czech art had a single aim — the creation of space of a new optic quality. Everything that has been written here about the character of Czech art can be considered from this sole fundamental tendency. It was the age old abstraction, prehistoric in origin but even in pre-Christian times permeating every creative process, that Czech art opposed. This struggle was fought out so that form might grow from man's sensual experience of life. The strivings of Czech style are thus connected to this struggle, in their spiritual aspects as well as in the particularities of form and composition. While attacking the abstract conception of form, Czech art attacks the objective order itself, whereby form was stylistically fettered, its collective obligation and absolute validity. The result is that the original purpose of the tectonic member falls into oblivion, its former logical reasoned shape is darkened and its forms are given quite another sense, completely different from the original. The tectonic form is first of all abandoned and the complex construction of the building simplified. Soon, however, this initial escape from the captivity of cold objectivity of the classical school leads to an open revolt when art begins to oppose the consistent logic and definite discipline in form caused by such an escape, and when all that was previously unimpeachable is intentionally abandoned. Czech art in expression and composition ultimately acquired the character of intentional and deliberate negation, manifesting itself in forms in which the old order was caricatured openly in mocking terms, which are all the more effective the more they revived the old style. By means of such mockeries, man wanted to express at last that he is no longer interested in matter, which in physical and objective form had till then been in the forefront of his interest: Czech art treats form only in terms of visible reality.

At the close of the fourteenth century the whole intricate artistic apparatus established by the High Gothic school lies in ruins about us. Its inner essence, based on a logical system of functions is dead and the driving force of rational order upon the human minds is spent and misdirected. Artistic form, quitting its former safe structure, begins, by contrast, a new existence, obeying laws that are no longer derived from the world of reason, so alien to it, but which spring from the harmony of sensual perceptions. Beauty for beauty's sake now becomes the aim of art, bent on the creation of harmonious form that is both pleasing to the senses and aesthetically perfect. The emancipation of form and its liberation from the rational order led, however, rather naturally to relaxation of formal discipline and erected as sole criterion, the demand of sensual beauty. The need of truth and truthfulness no longer was met by rejecting the very substance of a play — the stimulus of things that do not exist in reality and the evocation of delusive ideas. As art freed itself from the firm and heavy hand of rationalism and began to serve so unstable and labile a world as that of imagination and dreams, the obstructions to the creation of fantasy which could no longer be oppressed by firm insistence on logicality were removed and logical discipline gave way to improvisation — the artistically intentional illusions which reckon on a conscious deception of the spectator, were the consequence of it.

The artistic task of that unreal element in which the architect realizes his conceptions, the space, became greater with the increasing interest in unreal forms. Suddenly space gains in importance even at the expense of matter: it rejects massive proportion and cramping walls, dependence upon mechanics of vaulting construction and is ultimately transformed into unabstract space comprehended at a single sight, unexpressive but picturesque at the same time and existing as a part of subjective sensual space.

Artistic work springs now from a different psychic basis than that of the past. It does not exist for its own sake alone, without feeling the necessity of a spectator, as in the High Gothic, nor does it attempt to conquer or overpower him by the expressively directed system of forms tending to imaginary aim within the transcendental world, as in the post-classic period, but it attemps to evoke an emotionally parallel and psychically homogeneous conception in him and to excite him sensually. It, therefore, attacks his emotional instincts by way of his senses. In this way, of course, another part of the human spirit is set free which has up to now been suppressed by the rational order. Everything that is based on firm construction by reason and logic lays claim to absolute valitidy and excludes variations. The constructivist calculation can have but a single correct result to which everyone must independently arrive, without discriminations as to temperament and regardless of nationality, for it is simply identical in meaning. So artistic work, based on the rationalist use of function was synonymous and, therefore, universal: as soon as it left this basis and found itself on the slippery slope of feeling and improvisation it lost its absolute validity and became a subjectively comprehensible thing. Mood and emotional excitement which artistic work endeavoured to evoke in the spectator are unusually variable values, dependent on personal disposition and emotional potential; art loses its universal validity and becomes a subjective experience of the individual. Since Czech Gothic the individuality of modern man left the collective group and claimed its rights: we are as a matter of fact already standing on the threshold of modern time.

34. Kutná Hora; triple nave of St. James's with springing of the vaulting shafts, c. 1370.

35. Nymburk; side aisle of the deanery church; springing of the vaulting shafts. c. 1360.

36. Kutná Hora; the choir of the Church of Saint Mary "Na Náměti", springing of the vaulting shaft, c. 1370.

37. Karlštejn; St. Catherine's Chapel, springing of the vault, 1357.

38. Karlštejn; St. Catherine's Chapel, vault, 1357.

39. Prague; console supporting the nave vault in the Church of St. Apollinaris, c. 1370.

40. Vysoké Mýto; console supporting the vault of the vestry of the deanery church, c. 1370.

41. Prague; St. Vitus Cathedral. Parler's console supporting the vault on the eastern wall of the vestry, before 1360.

42. Litomyšl; vestry of the Augustinian Monastery, springing of the vault, 1360—1370.

43. Prague; choir of the Church of St. Martin's in the Wall, 1370—1380.

44. Litomyšl; vestry of the Augustinian Monastery, 1360—1370.

45. Prague; St. Vitus Cathedral. Parler's vault over the south narthex, reconstructed by K. Hilbert. Plan anterior to 1368.

46. Prague; St. Vitus Cathedral. Parler's vault over the southern narthex reconstructed by K. Hilbert. Plan anterior to 1368.

47. Vysoké Mýto; southern narthex of the deanery church, view of the vault, 1370—1380.

48. Sadská; vaults of the church choir, 1370—1380.

49. Castle Lipnice; vault of the entrance hall, after 1370.

50. Prague; choir of the Church of St. Martin's in the Wall. Vault, 1370—1380.

51. Plzeň; vault of the vestry of All Saints' Church, c. 1380.

52. Nymburk; deanery church. Vault under the south tower, 1375—1380.

53. Nymburk; deanery church; console supporting the vault under the south tower, 1375—1380.

54. Prague; St. Vitus Cathedral. Parler's console of the choir pier behind the high altar, c. 1370.

55. Vysoké Mýto; console supporting the baldachin in the south narthex of the deanery church, c. 1370—1380.

56. Prague; west narthex of the Saint Mary in Catenis, 1370—1380.

57. Castle Lipnice; the springing of the vault over the entrance hall, after 1370.

58. Plzeň; southern ambit of the Franciscan monastery, c. 1370—1380.

59. Plzeň; the choir of the Church of All Saints, 1370—1380.

60. Nymburk; south tower of the deanery church, 1375—1380.

61. Nymburk; deanery church. Choir, 1280—1290; basilican triple nave, 1350—1360; south tower, 1375—1380; south narthex about 1510.

62. Skuteč; parish church. Console supporting the vault in the choir, c. 1370

63. Prague; northern double nave in the church of St. Castulus, before 1375.

64. Jaroměř; console supporting the vault under the choir in the minster, c. 1410.

65. Slavětín; springing of the vault in the choir 1375.

66. Prague; northern double nave of the church of St. Castulus, before 1375.

67. Prague; northern double nave of the church of St. Castulus, before 1375.

68. Prague; western double nave, ambit adjoining St. James's Monastery, before 1374.

69. Vetlá; nave of the church, c. 1370.

70. Vetlá; vault in the church nave, c. 1370.

71. Vetlá; vault in the church nave. cč 1370

72. Jindřichův Hradec; pillar base in the Chapel of St. Nicholas, c. 1365.

73. Jindřichův Hradec; central pier in the Chapel of St. Nicholas, c. 1365.

74. Třeboň; south part of the ambit, 1370—1380.

75. Jindřichův Hradec; Chapel of St. Nicholas, c. 1365.

76. Třeboň; double nave of the minster, c. 1380.

77. Třeboň; double nave of the minster, c. 1380.

78. Jindřichův Hradec; triple nave of the same height in the deanery church, c. 1370—1380.

79. Třeboň; vaults of the double nave in the minster, shortly after 1380.

80. Soběslav; double nave Church of St. Vitus, after 1375.

81. Soběslav; Church of St. Vitus, after 1375.

82. Sedlčany; deanery church. Tower and partly also the stonework of the nave c. 1270. The choir and double nave after 1375.

83. Bavorov; the choir and tower of the deanery church, c. 1375.

84. Třeboň; small southern portal of the double nave minster, c. 1375.

85. Jindřichův Hradec; south portal in the nave of the deanery church, after 1375.

86. Budějovice; north-east corner of the ambit in the Dominican Monastery, c. 1370. (Window tracery, c. 1500.)

87. Jindřichův Hradec; chapter-house of the Minorite monastery, c. 1375.

88. Soběslav; double nave church of St. Vitus. Vaults after 1375.

89. Soběslav; double nave church of St. Vitus. Vaults after 1375.

90. Sedlčany; the choir of the deanery church, after 1375.

91. Kondrac; church choir, 1375—1380.

92. Prague; west facade of the church of Saint Mary in front of Týn. Central window, main part of the gallery and gable date from about 1390; towers from the second half of the 15th and beginning of the 16th century.

93. Prague; Carolinum. Oriel window of the Chapel of the University Aula, after 1390.

94. Prague; Carolinum, oriel window of the Chapel of the University Aula, corbels and supporting consoles, after 1390.

95. Libiš; church, c. 1385—1390.

96. Sezemice; the choir of the north chapel, 1380—1390.

97. Libiš; vaulting console in the choir, 1385—1390.

98. Libiš; vaulting console in the choir, c. 1385—1390.

99. Sezemice; vault over the nave of the north chapel, 1380—1390.

100. Prague; springing of the Parler's vault in the Old Town Bridge Tower, 1380—1390.

101. Prague; church of St. Apollinaris. Base of the north portal, c. 1370.

102. Bavorov; deanery church. Base of the south portal, c. 1385.

103. Bavorov; deanery church. South portal, c. 1385.

104. Soběslav; deanery church of St. Peter. South portal of the nave, c. 1380—1385.

105. Miličín; parish church, west portal of the nave, c. 1380.

106. Bavorov; deanery church. Sedilia in the presbytery, c. 1370.

107. Miličín; parish church, c. 1380. 15th century (1417).

108. Němčice; parish church, c. 1385—1390, older walls incorporated into the nave date from about 1260.

109. Velká Blánice; parish church, c. 1385—1390, older walls incorporated into the nave date from about 1280.

110. Nezamyslice; parish church. The choir dates from about 1390.

111. Nezamyslice; parish church. The choir dates from about 1390.

112. Soběslav; deanery church of St. Peter, c. 1380—1385, with the 15th century tower.

113. Němčice; parish church. Vaults over the double nave, c. 1385—1390.

114. Němčice; parish church, c. 1385—1390, older walls incorporated into the nave date from 1260.

115. Vyšší Brod; triple nave of the abbey church, 1360—1380.

116. Soběslav; deanery church of St. Peter. Outside walls of the choir and nave with the triumphal arch, c. 1380—1385. Vaults of the choir and nave date from the end of the 15th century.

117. Kutná Hora; Church of the Holy Trinity. Vaults of the triple nave date from the beginning of the 15th century (1417?).

118. Kutná Hora; Church of the Holy Trinity. Triple nave dates from the beginning of the 15th century (1417?).

119. Kutná Hora; Church of the Holy Trinity. Triple nave dates from the beginning of the 15th century (1417?).

120. Sedlec; ossuary. About 1400.

121. Loučeň; parish church, c. 1400.

122. Sedlec; ossuary, interior, c. 1400.

123. Sedlec; ossuary, about 1400.

124. Milevsko; parish church of St. Giles. Vault of the choir, c. 1390.

125. Milevsko; parish church of St. Giles. Vault of the choir, c. 1390.

126. Milevsko; parish church of St. Giles. The choir and torso of the double nave vault, c. 1390.

127. Milevsko; the choir of St. Giles, parish church, c. 1390.

128. Krumlov; castle. Former vestry of the castle chapel, c. 1430—1440.

129. Krumlov; castle. Vaulted hall behind the east tower, c. 1430—1440.

130. Krumlov; deanery church of St. Vitus. Small porch 1440, opening on to the north aisle, c. 1430.

131. Suchdol; parish church. Vaults of the choir and the triple nave, c. 1440.

132. Prague; St. Vitus Cathedral. Parler's vault over the choir, 1386.

133. Krumlov; deanery church of St. Vitus. Vault of the triple nave, and the choir, 1407—1439.

134. Krumlov; deanery church of St. Vitus. Triple nave, 1407—1439.

135. Krumlov; deanery church of St. Vitus. Triple nave, 1407—1439.

136. Krumlov; deanery church of St. Vitus, 1407—1439.

137. Krumlov; deanery church of St. Vitus, 1407—1439.

138. Krumlov; deanery church of St. Vitus. South arcades of the triple nave, 1407—1439.

139. Krumlov; deanery church of St. Vitus. Triumphal arch and the first arcade separating the nave from the north aisle, 1407—1439.

140. Suchdol; parish church. Vault over the choir, c. 1400—1420.

141. Krumlov; deanery church of St. Vitus. Vault over the choir, 1407—1439.

142. Klatovy; deanery church. Vault over the choir, c. 1400—1410.

143. Klatovy; deanery church. Vault over the choir, c. 1400—1410.

144. Plzeň; archdeaconate church of St. Bartholomew. South portal, of the triple nave 1400—1420.

145. Litice; parish church. North portal, c. 1420.

146. Čéčovice; parish church. West façade, c. 1410.

147. Čéčovice; parish church, c. 1410.

148. Čéčovice; parish church. Doorway of the choir, c. 1410.

149. Dolní Kounice; vaulting shaft in the minster, c. 1400.

150. Dolní Kounice; vaulting schaft in the minster.

151. Panenský Týnec; minster. Left-side door-case of the south portal, c. 1410.

152. Panenský Týnec; minster. Detail from the left-side door-case of the south portal, c. 1410.

153. Castle Krakovec; vaulting console on the ground-floor level, c. 1380.

154. Castle Krakovec; vaulting console on the ground-floor level, c. 1380.

155. Castle Točník; vaulting console in the Great Hall of the Royal Palace, 1395—1400.

156. Castle Točník; vaulting console in the Great Hall of the Royal Palace, 1395—1400.

157. Castle Točník; 1395—1400.

158. Castle Točník; courtyard façade of the Royal Palace, 1395—1400.

159. Castle Krakovec; c. 1380.

160. Castle Točník; Great Hall of the Royal Palace, 1395—1400.

161. Castle Točník; vaulting consoles in the Great Hall of the Royal Palace, 1395—1400.

162. Prague Castle; the so-called Pillar Hall, c. 1400.

163. Prague Castle; the so-called Pillar Hall, c. 1400.

164. Prague Castle; vaulting consoles in the Pillar Hall, c. 1400.

165. Prague Castle; vaulting console in the Pillar Hall, c. 1400.

166. Prague Castle; vaulting console in the Pillar Hall, c. 1400.

167. Prague Castle; vaulting console in the Pillar Hall, c. 1400.

168. Kutná Hora; Oriel Chapel in the Italian Courtyard, 1400.

169. Kutná Hora; Oriel Chapel in the Italian Courtyard, 1400.

170. Kutná Hora; Italian Courtyard. Chapel vault, 1400.

171. Kutná Hora; oriel window of the Chapel in the Italian courtyard, 1400.

172. Kutná Hora; vaulting shaft in the Oriel Chapel, 1400.

173. Kutná Hora; vaulting shaft in the Oriel chapel, 1400.

174. Jaroměř; minster. Vault of the north choir, c. 1410.

175. Chrudim; deanery church. Vault over the north porch, c. 1400.

176. Dvůr Králové; parish church. Capital of the pier in the triple nave, c. 1400.

177. Chrudim; deanery church, friezes of the piers supporting the arcade in the nave, c. 1400.

178. Dvůr Králové; parish church, triple nave, c. 1400.

179. Dvůr Králové; parish church, triple nave, c. 1400.

180. Telč; church of St. James, 1443—1457.

181. Telč; parish church of St. James. Vault over the nave, 1443—1457.

182. Blatná; parish church. The choir, 1414—1444.

183. Plzeň; archdeaconate church of St. Bartholomew. Vault over the triple nave, c. 1480.

184. Bělčice; parish church. Diamond vaulting, 1515 (gilded strips at the angles of later date).

185. Soběslav; deanery church of St. Peter. Diamond vault over the nave, 1499—1501.

186. Soběslav; deanery church of St. Peter. Diamond vault over the nave, 1499—1501.

REPRODUCTIONS

1. Plzeň; archdeacon's church of St. Bartholomew. Nave, aisles with towers date from about 1330, presbytery from 1350–60, window tracery from the third quarter of the 15th cent.

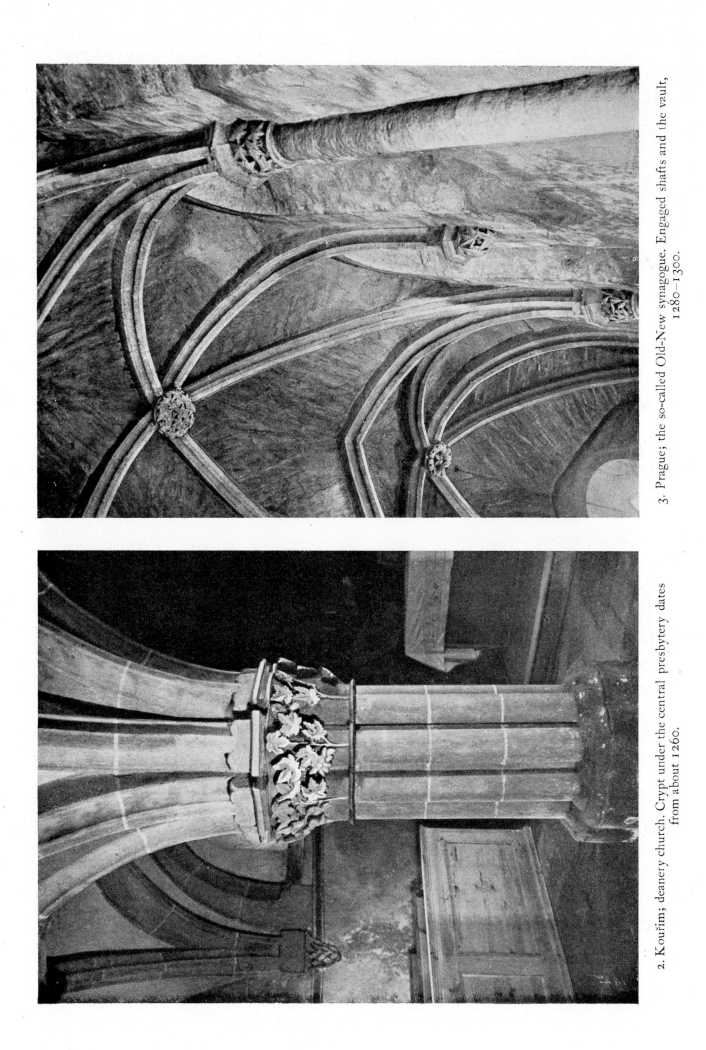

3. Prague; the so-called Old-New synagogue. Engaged shafts and the vault, 1280–1300.

2. Kouřim; deanery church. Crypt under the central presbytery dates from about 1260.

5. Kutná Hora; presbytery of St. James's, c. 1330.

4. Prague; presbytery in the minster of Saint Mary of-the-Snow, according to a plan from the middle of the 14th cent.

7. Kutná Hora; presbytery of St. James's, c. 1330.

6. Kutná Hora; exterior of the presbytery of St. James's, c. 1330.

9. Kutná Hora; presbytery of St. James's, keystone of the vault, c. 1330.

8. Kutná Hora; presbytery of St. James's, the vaulting shafts, c. 1330.

11. Prague; minster of St. Anne, console supporting the nave vault, c. 1330.

10. Sázava; chapter-house, base of the central pier, c. 1340.

13. Prague; chapel adjoining the presbytery in the minster of St. James's, c. 1330

12. Sázava; chapter-house, keystones of the vaults, c. 1340.

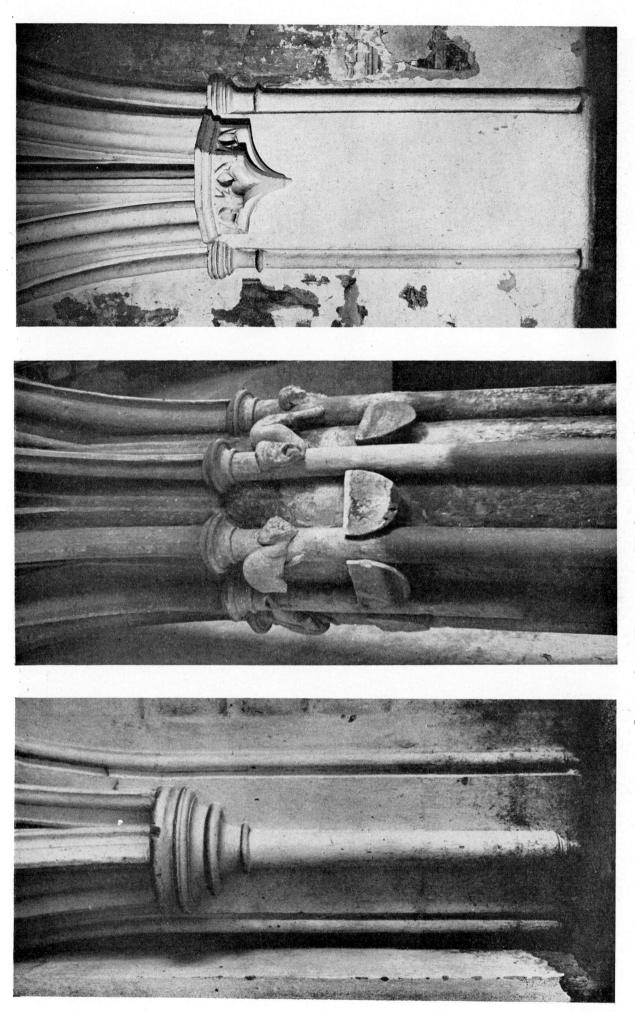

14. Sázava; chapter-house, engaged shaft sand capital of the central pier, c. 1340.

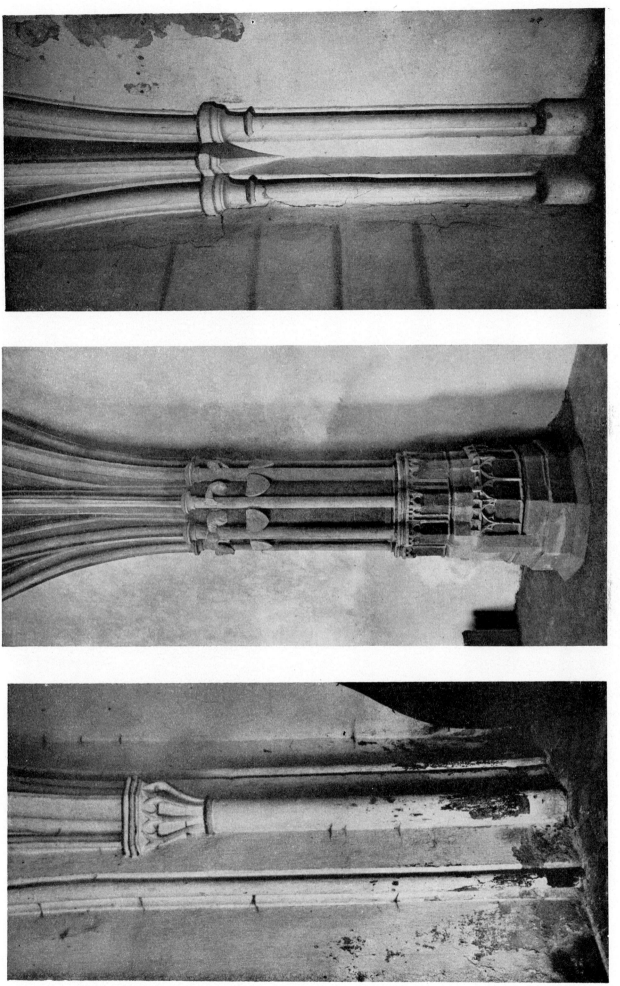

15. Sázava; chapter-house, wall, corner shaft and the central pier, c. 1340.

16. Kutná Hora; triple nave of the same height in St. James's, c. 1370.

17. Plzeň; basilican triple nave of the Franciscan church. Triumphal arch c. 1300; arcades dividing the nave from the aisles, c. 1340.

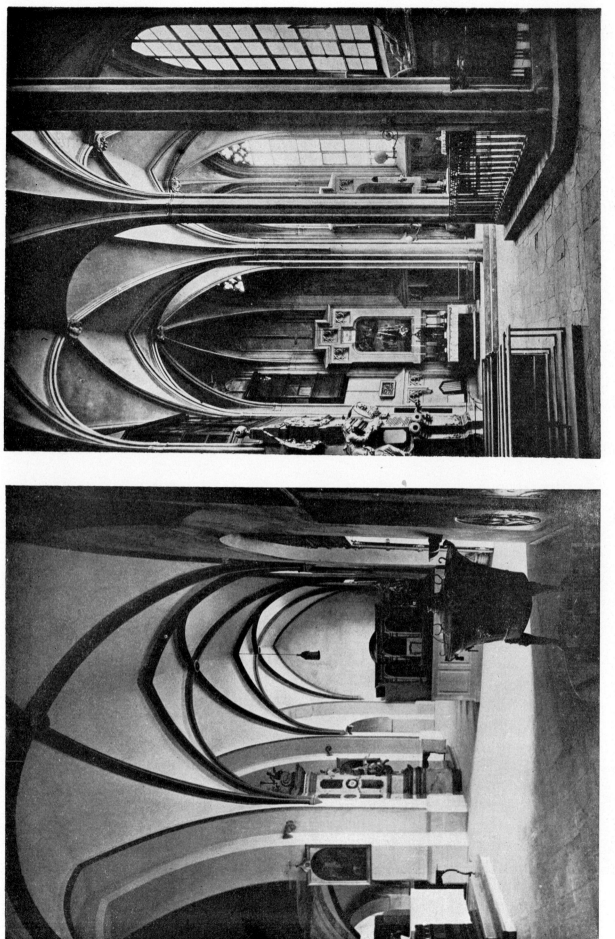

19. Vienna; double nave of St. George's chapel adjoining the Augustinian Church, c. 1330.

18. Prague; northern side aisle in St. Stephen's, 1350–1360.

21. Nymburk; deanery church, side aisle, c. 1350–1360.

20. Nepomuk; deanery church of St. James's, side aisle, c. 1360–1370.

22. Plzeň; triple nave of the Franciscan church. View of the arcades of the south aisle looking toward the nave, c. 1340.

24. Prague; site of the former double nave Church of the Holy Ghost, c. 1360.

23. Kutná Hora; Church of Saint Mary „na Náměti",
the arcades seen from the south aisle, c. 1370.

26. Prague; Church of St. Apollinaris, c. 1370.

25. Kutná Hora; deanery church of St. James's triple nave, side aisles and towers, c. 1370.

28. Prague; Church of Saint Mary on-the-Green, nave vault.
Outside walls with vaulting shafts, c. 1360–1370. Vault with the central
pier is the post-Hussite copy of the original vault.

27. Prague; Church of Saint Mary on-the-Green, presbytery, 1360–1370.

29. Prague; Church of St. Apollinaris, c. 1370.

30. Prague; Church of Saint Mary on-the-Green, c. 1360-1370.

32. Prague; Church of Saint Mary on-the-Green, view of the presbytery, 1360–1370.

31. Prague; vaulting shafts in the presbytery of the Church of St. Apollinaris, c. 1370.

34. Kutná Hora; triple nave of St. James's with springing of the vaulting shafts, c. 1370.

33. Kolín; Parler's presbytery in the Church of St. Bartholomew, with springing of the vaulting shafts, c. 1370.

36. Kutná Hora; presbytery of the Church of Saint Mary „na Náměti“, springing of the vaulting shaft, c. 1370.

35. Nymburk; side aisle of the deanery church; springing of the vaulting shafts, c. 1360.

38. Karlštejn; St. Catherine's Chapel, vault, 1357.

37. Karlštejn; St. Catherine's Chapel, springing of the vault, 1357.

40. Vysoké Mýto; console supporting the vault of the vestry of the deanery church, c. 1370.

39. Prague; console supporting the nave vault in the Church of St. Apollinaris, c. 1370.

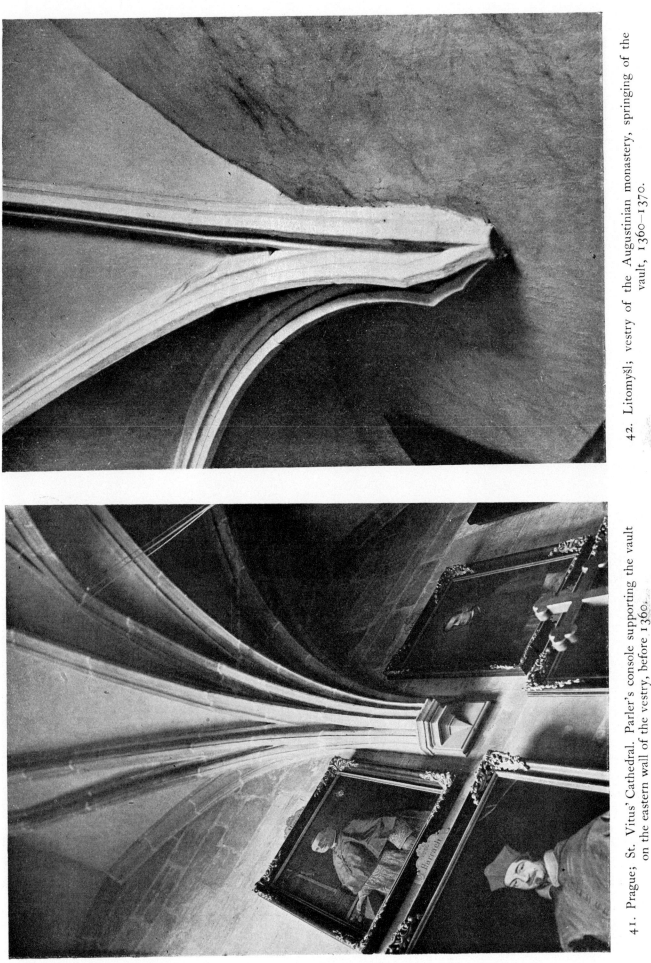

42. Litomyšl; vestry of the Augustinian monastery, springing of the vault, 1360–1370.

41. Prague; St. Vitus' Cathedral. Parler's console supporting the vault on the eastern wall of the vestry, before 1360.

43. Prague; presbytery of the Church of St. Martin's in the Wall, 1370–1380.

44. Litomyšl; vestry of the Augustinian Monastery, 1360–1370.

45. Prague; St. Vitus' Cathedral. Parler's vault over the south narthex, reconstructed by K. Hilbert.
Plan anterior to 1368.

46. Prague; St. Vitus' Cathedral. Parler's vault over the southern narthex reconstructed by K. Hilbert. Plan anterior to 1368.

47. Vysoké Mýto; southern narthex of the deanery church, view of the vault, 1370–1380.

48. Sadská; vaults of the church presbytery, 1370–1380.

49. Castle Lipnice; vault of the entrance hall, after 1370.

50. Prague; presbytery of the Church of St. Martin's in the Wall. Vault, 1370–1380.

51. Plzeň; vault of the vestry of All Saints' Church, c. 1380.

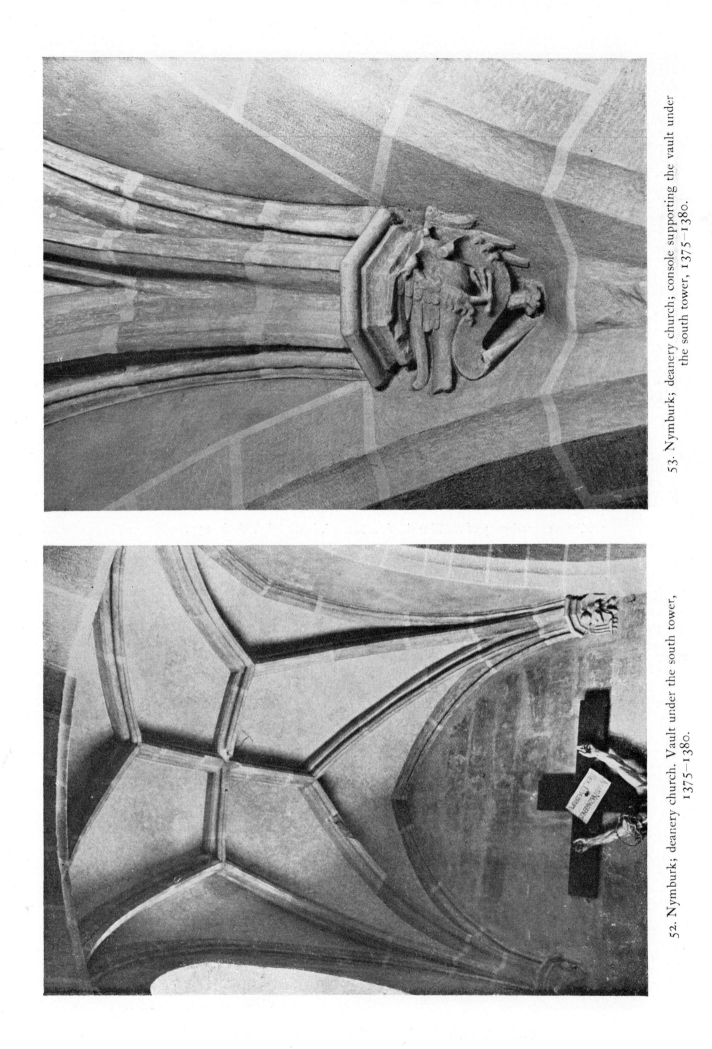

53. Nymburk; deanery church; console supporting the vault under the south tower, 1375–1380.

52. Nymburk; deanery church. Vault under the south tower, 1375–1380.

55. Vysoké Mýto; console supporting the baldachin in the south narthex of the deanery church, c. 1370–1380.

54. Prague; St. Vitus' Cathedral. Parler's console of the choir pier behind the high altar, c. 1370.

57. Castle Lipnice; the springing of the vault over the entrance hall, after 1370.

56. Prague; west narthex of the Saint Mary in Catenis, 1370–1380.

59. Plzeň; presbytery of the Church of All Saints, 1370—1380.

58. Plzeň; southern ambit of the Franciscan monastery, c. 1370—1380.

60. Nymburk; south tower of the deanery church, 1375–1380.

61. Nymburk; deanery church. Presbytery, 1280–1290; basilican triple nave, 1350–1360; south tower, 1375–1380; south narthex about 1510.

63. Prague; northern double nave in the church of St. Haštal, before 1375.

62. Skuteč; parish church. Console supporting the vault in the presbytery, c. 1370.

65. Slavětín; springing of the vault in the presbytery, 1375.

64. Jaroměř; console supporting the vault under the choir in the minster, c. 1410.

66. Prague; northern double nave of the church of St. Haštal, before 1375.

67. Prague; northern double nave of the church of St. Haštal, before 1375.

68. Prague; western double nave, ambit adjoining St. James's monastery, before 1374.

69. Vetlá; nave of the church, c. 1370.

71. Vetlá; vault in the church nave, c. 1370.

70. Vetlá; vault in the church nave, c. 1370.

73. Jindřichův Hradec; central pier in the Chapel of St. Nicholas, c. 1365.

72. Jindřichův Hradec; pillar base in the Chapel of St. Nicholas, c. 1365.

74. Třeboň; south part of the ambit, 1370—1380.

75. Jindřichův Hradec; Chapel of St. Nicholas, c. 1365.

76. Třeboň; double nave of the minster, c. 1380.

77. Třeboň; double nave of the minster, c. 1380.

78. Jindřichův Hradec; triple nave of the same height in the deanery church, c. 1370-80.

79. Třeboň; vaults of the double nave in the minster, shortly after 1380.

80. Soběslav; double nave Church of St. Vitus, after 1375.

81. Soběslav; Church of St. Vitus, after 1375.

83. Bavorov; presbytery and tower of the deanery church, c. 1375.

82. Sedlčany; deanery church. Tower and partly also the stonework of the nave c. 1270. Presbytery and double nave, after 1375.

85. Jindřichův Hradec; south portal in the nave of the deanery church, after 1375.

84. Třeboň; small southern portal of the double nave minster, c. 1375.

87. Jindřichův Hradec; chapter-house of the Minorite monastery, c. 1375.

86. Budějovice; north-east corner of the ambit in the Dominican monastery, c. 1370. (Window tracery, c. 1500).

89. Soběslav; double nave church of St. Vitus. Vaults after 1375.

88. Soběslav; double nave church of St. Vitus. Vaults after 1375.

90. Sedlčany; presbytery of the deanery church, after 1375.

91. Kondrac; church presbytery, 1375–1380.

92. Prague; west facade of the church of Saint Mary in front of Týn. Central window, main part of the gallery and gable date from about 1390; towers from the second half of the 15th and beginning of the 16th century.

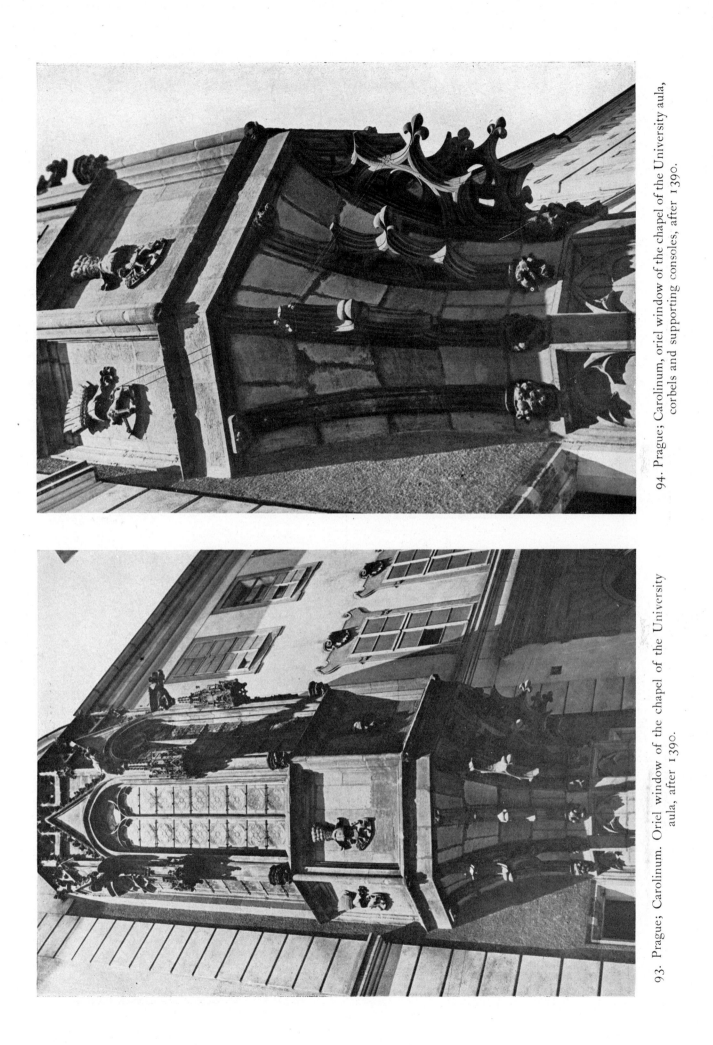

94. Prague; Carolinum, oriel window of the chapel of the University aula, corbels and supporting consoles, after 1390.

93. Prague; Carolinum. Oriel window of the chapel of the University aula, after 1390.

96. Sezemice; presbytery of the north chapel, 1380–1390.

95. Libiš; church, c. 1385–1390.

98. Libiš; vaulting console in the presbytery, c. 1385–1390.

97. Libiš; vaulting console in the presbytery, 1385–1390.

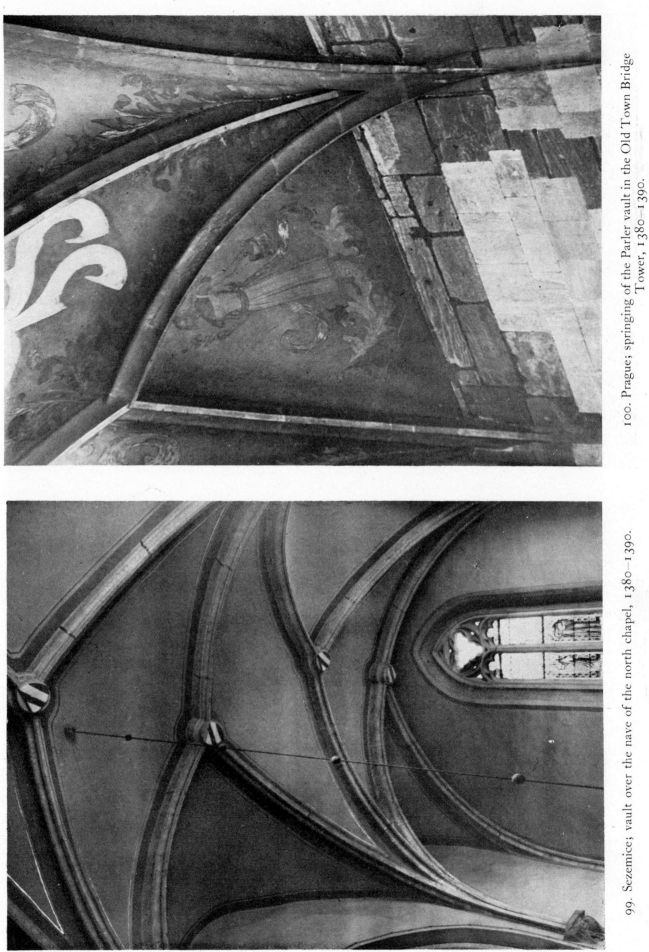

100. Prague; springing of the Parler vault in the Old Town Bridge Tower, 1380—1390.

99. Sezemice; vault over the nave of the north chapel, 1380—1390.

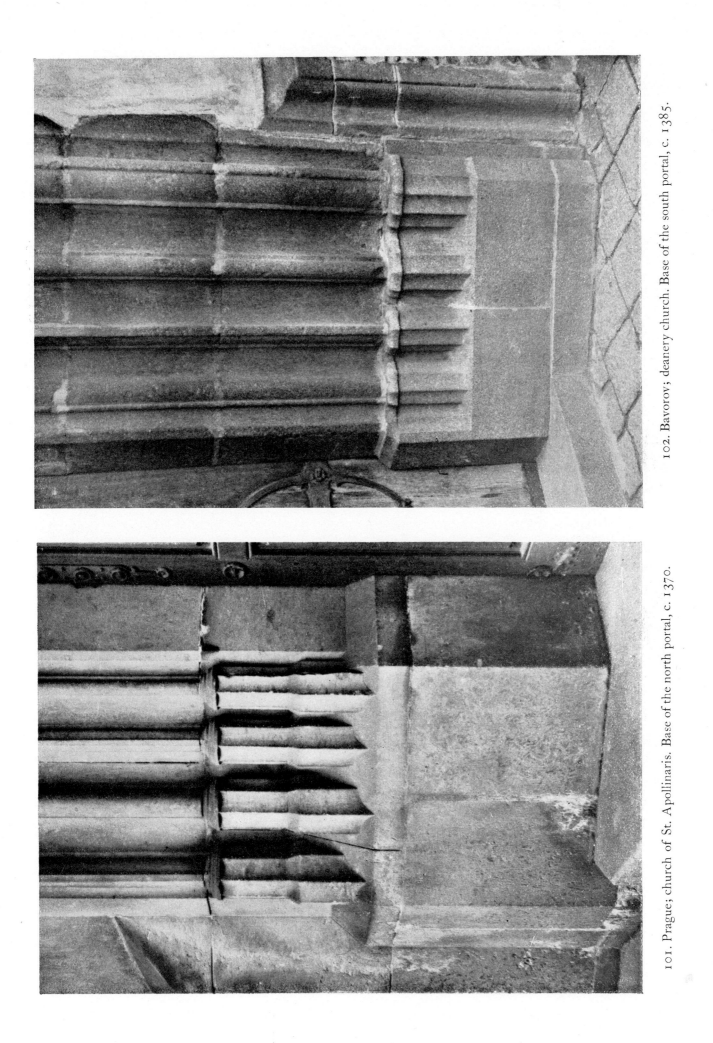

102. Bavorov; deanery church. Base of the south portal, c. 1385.

101. Prague; church of St. Apollinaris. Base of the north portal, c. 1370.

104. Soběslav; deanery church of St. Peter. South portal of the nave,
c. 1380–1385.

103. Bavorov; deanery church. South portal, c. 1385.

106. Bavorov; deanery church. Sedilia in the presbytery, c. 1370.

105. Milíčín; parish church, west portal of the nave, c. 1380.

108. Němčice; parish church, c. 1385–1390, older walls incorporated into the nave date from about 1260.

107. Milíčín; parish church, c. 1380.

110. Nezamyslice; parish church. Presbytery dates from about 1390.

109. Velká Blánice; parish church, c. 1385–1390, older walls incorporated into the nave date from about 1280.

111. Nezamyslice; parish church. Presbytery dates from about 1390.

112. Soběslav; deanery church of St. Peter, c. 1380–1385, with the 15th century tower.

113. Němčice; parish church. Vaults over the double nave, c. 1385–1390.

114. Němčice; parish church, c. 1385–1390, older walls incorporated into the nave date from about 1260.

115. Vyšší Brod; triple nave of the abbey church, 1360–1380.

116. Soběslav; deanery church of St. Peter. Outside walls of the presbytery and nave with the triumphal arch, c. 1380–1385. Vaults of the presbytery and nave date from the end of the 15th century.

117. Kutná Hora; Church of the Holy Trinity. Vaults of the triple nave date from the beginning of the 15th century (1417?).

118. Kutná Hora; Church of the Holy Trinity. Triple nave dates from the beginning
of the 15th century (1417?).

119. Kutná Hora; Church of the Holy Trinity. Triple nave dates from the beginning of the 15th century (1417?).

120. Sedlec; charnel house. About 1400.

121. Loučeň; parish church, c. 1400.

123. Sedlec; charnel-house, about 1400.

122. Sedlec; charnel-house, interior, c. 1400.

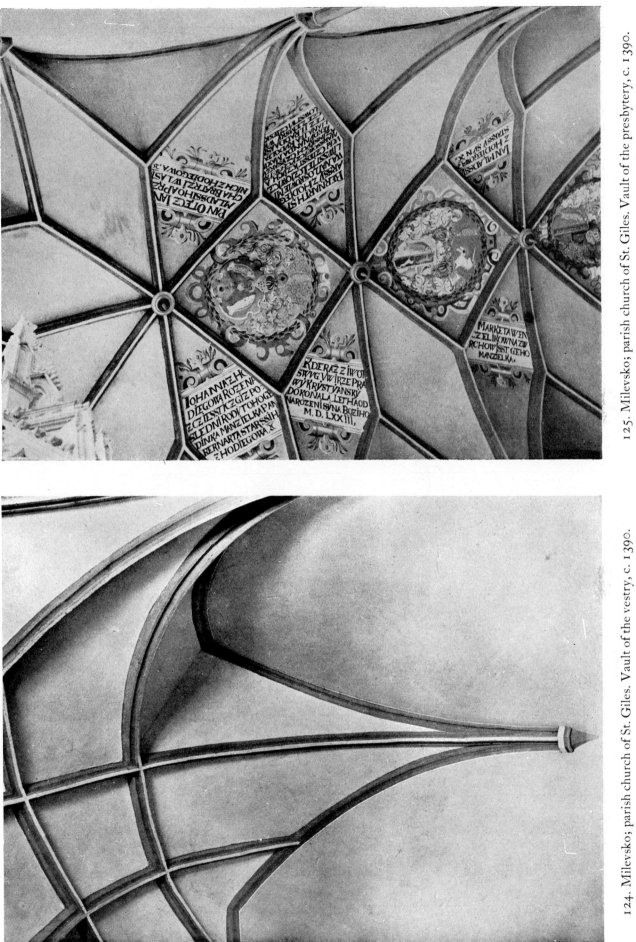

125. Milevsko; parish church of St. Giles. Vault of the presbytery, c. 1390.

124. Milevsko; parish church of St. Giles. Vault of the vestry, c. 1390.

126. Milevsko; parish church of St. Giles. Presbytery and torso of the double nave vault, c. 1390.

127. Milevsko; presbytery of St. Giles's parish church, c. 1390.

128. Krumlov; castle. Former vestry of the castle chapel, c. 1430–1440.

129. Krumlov; castle. Vaulted hall behind the east tower, c. 1430–1440.

130. Krumlov; deanery church of St. Vitus. Small porch 1440, opening on to the north aisle, c. 1430.

131. Suchdol; parish church. Vaults of the presbytery and the triple nave, c. 1440.

132. Prague; St. Vitus' Cathedral. Parler's vault over the presbytery, 1386.

133. Krumlov; deanery church of St. Vitus. Vault of the triple nave, and the presbytery, 1407—1439.

134. Krumlov; deanery church of St. Vitus. Triple nave, 1407–1439.

135. Krumlov; deanery church of St. Vitus. Triple nave, 1407–1439.

136. Krumlov; deanery church of St. Vitus, 1407–1439.

137. Krumlov; deanery church of St. Vitus, 1407–1439.

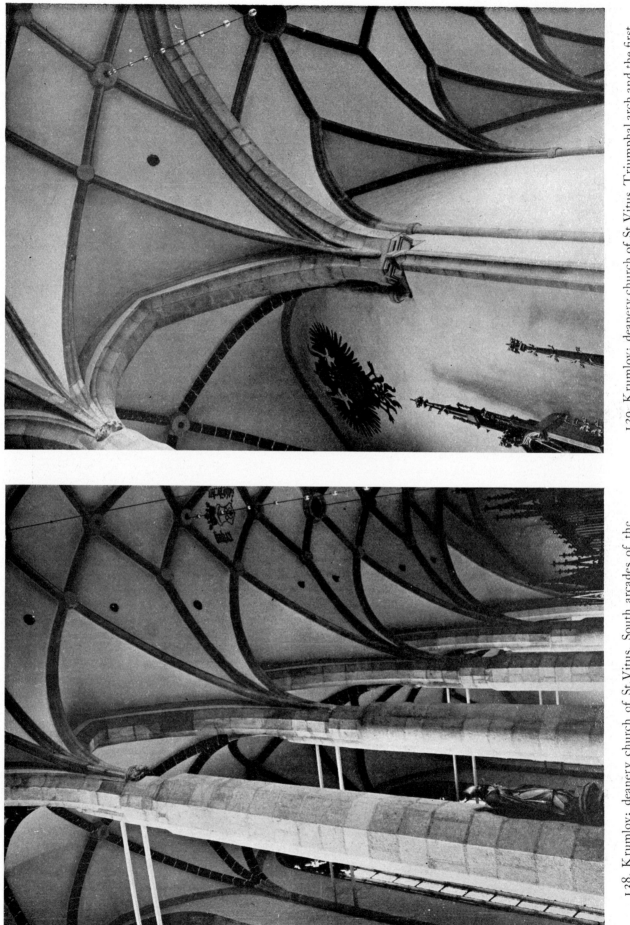

139. Krumlov; deanery church of St. Vitus. Triumphal arch and the first arcade separating the nave from the north aisle, 1407–1439.

138. Krumlov; deanery church of St. Vitus. South arcades of the triple nave, 1407–1439.

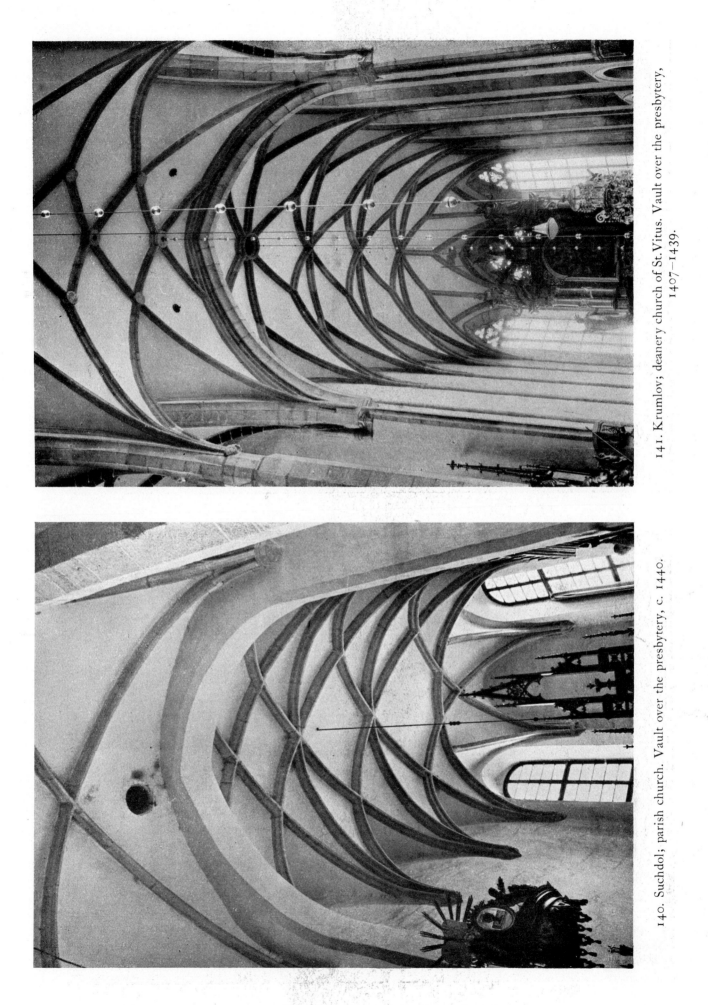

141. Krumlov; deanery church of St. Vitus. Vault over the presbytery, 1407—1439.

140. Suchdol; parish church. Vault over the presbytery, c. 1440.

143. Klatovy; deanery church. Vault over the presbytery, c. 1400–1410.

142. Klatovy; deanery church. Vault over the presbytery, c. 1400–1410.

144. Plzeň; archdeacon's church of St. Bartholomew. South portal,
of the triple nave 1400–1420.

145. Litice; parish church. North portal, c. 1420.

147. Čéčovice; parish church, c. 1410.

146. Čéčovice; parish church. West façade, c. 1410.

148. Čéčovice; parish church. Doorway of the choir, c. 1410.

150. Dolní Kounice; vaulting shaft in the minster.

149. Dolní Kounice; vaulting shaft in the minster, c. 1400.

152. Panenský Týnec; minster. Detail from the left-side door-case of the south portal, c. 1410.

151. Panenský Týnec; minster. Left-side door-case of the south portal, c. 1410.

153. Castle Krakovec; vaulting console on the ground-floor level, c. 1380.

154. Castle Krakovec; vaulting console on the ground-floor level, c. 1380.

156. Castle Točník; vaulting console in the Great Hall of the Royal
Palace, 1395–1400.

155. Castle Točník; vaulting console in the Great Hall of the Royal
Palace, 1395–1400.

157. Castle Točník, 1395–1400.

158. Castle Točník; courtyard facade of the Royal Palace, 1395–1400.

159. Castle Krakovec, c. 1380.

160. Castle Točník; Great Hall of the Royal Palace, 1395–1400.

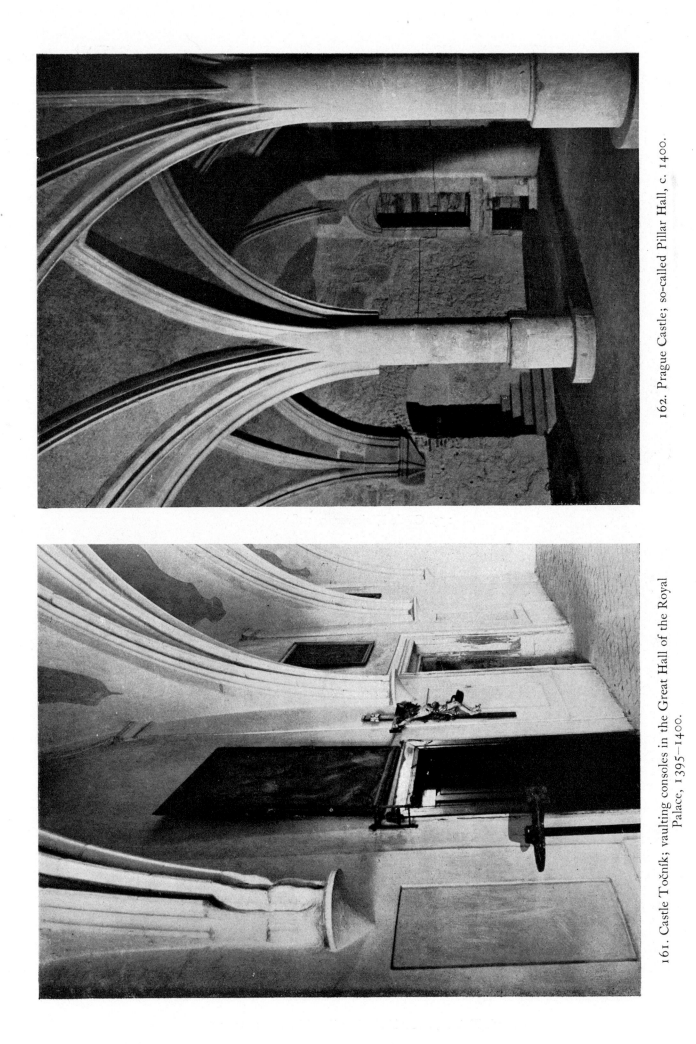

162. Prague Castle; so-called Pillar Hall, c. 1400.

161. Castle Točník; vaulting consoles in the Great Hall of the Royal
Palace, 1395–1400.

163. Prague Castle; so-called Pillar Hall, c. 1400.

165. Prague Castle; vaulting console in the Pillar Hall, c. 1400.

164. Prague Castle; vaulting consoles in the Pillar Hall, c. 1400.

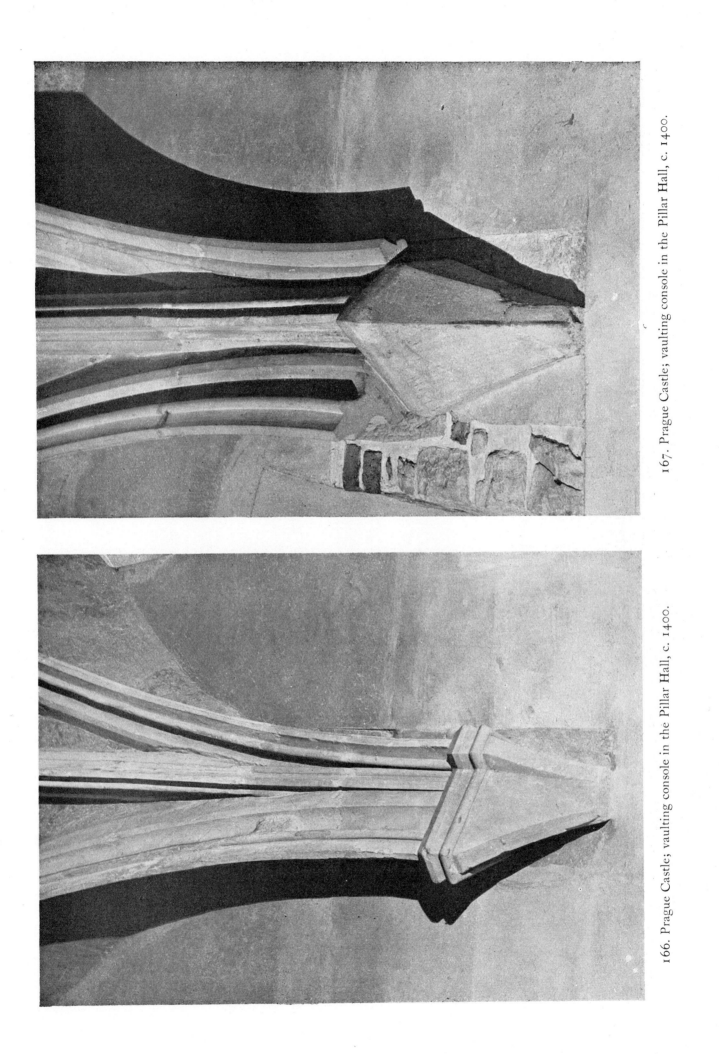

167. Prague Castle; vaulting console in the Pillar Hall, c. 1400.

166. Prague Castle; vaulting console in the Pillar Hall, c. 1400.

168. Kutná Hora; oriel chapel in the Italian Courtyard, 1400.

169. Kutná Hora; oriel chapel in the Italian Courtyard, 1400.

171. Kutná Hora; oriel window of the chapel in the Italian courtyard, 1400.

170. Kutná Hora; Italian courtyard. Chapel vault, 1400.

173. Kutná Hora; vaulting shaft in the oriel chapel, 1400.

172. Kutná Hora; vaulting shaft in the oriel chapel, 1400.

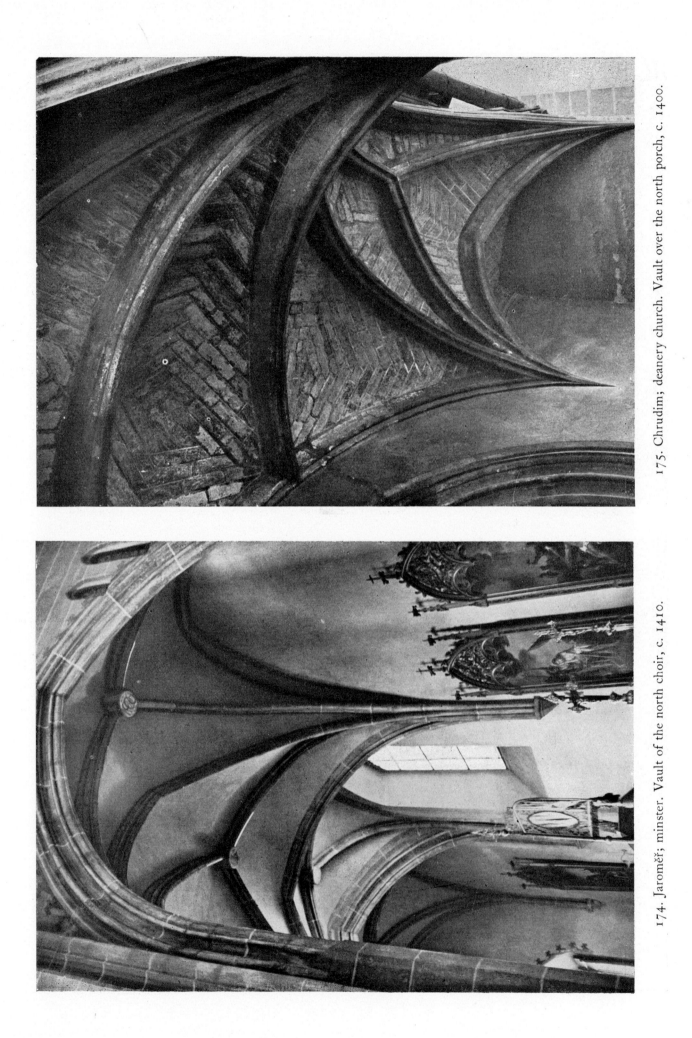

175. Chrudim; deanery church. Vault over the north porch, c. 1400.

174. Jaroměř; minster. Vault of the north choir, c. 1410.

177. Chrudim; deanery church, friezes of the piers supporting the arcade in the nave, c. 1400.

176. Dvůr Králové; parish church. Capital of the pier in the triple nave, c. 1400.

178. Dvůr Králové; parish church, triple nave, c. 1400.

179. Dvůr Králové; parish church, triple nave, c. 1400.

180. Telč; church of St. James, 1443–1457.

181. Telč; parish church of St. James. Vault over the nave, 1443–1457.

182. Blatná; parish church. Presbytery, 1414–1444.

183. Plzeň; archdeacon's church of St. Bartholomew. Vault over the triple nave, c. 1480.

184. Bělčice; parish church. Diamond vault nave, 1515 (gilded strips at the angles of later date.)

185. Soběslav; deanery church of St. Peter. Diamond vault over the nave, 1499–1501.

186. Soběslav; deanery church of St. Peter. Diamond vault over the nave, 1499—1501.